MAKE YOUR OWN CREATIVE

SCRAPBOOK
PAGES

MAKE YOUR OWN CREATIVE

SCRAPBOOK PAGES

Keep your treasured memories alive with this practical, step-by-step
project book, beautifully illustrated with over 600 colour photographs

Featuring more than 60 inspired album pages and covers, display boards,
celebration cards, heritage quilts, keepsake boxes and concertina books

ALISON LINDSAY

southwater

Dedication
For Paul and Emily

This edition is published by Southwater,
an imprint of Anness Publishing Ltd,
Hermes House, 88–89 Blackfriars Road, London SE1 8HA;
tel. 020 7401 2077; fax 020 7633 9499
www.southwaterbooks.com; www.annesspublishing.com

If you like the images in this book and would like to investigate using them for publishing, promotions or advertising,
please visit our website www.practicalpictures.com for more information.

UK agent: The Manning Partnership Ltd; tel. 01225 478444; fax 01225 478440; sales@manning-partnership.co.uk
UK distributor: Grantham Book Services Ltd; tel. 01476 541080; fax 01476 541061; orders@gbs.tbs-ltd.co.uk
North American agent/distributor: National Book Network; tel. 301 459 3366; fax 301 429 5746; www.nbnbooks.com
Australian agent/distributor: Pan Macmillan Australia; tel. 1300 135 113; fax 1300 135 103;
customer.service@macmillan.com.au
New Zealand agent/distributor: David Bateman Ltd; tel. (09) 415 7664; fax (09) 415 8892

Publisher: Joanna Lorenz
Editorial Director: Helen Sudell
Project Editors: Ann Kay, Simona Hill and Emma Clegg
Designer: Terry Jeavons
Photographers: Mark Wood and Paul Bricknell
Production Controller: Claire Rae

ETHICAL TRADING POLICY

At Anness Publishing we believe that business should be conducted in an ethical and ecologically sustainable way, with respect for the environment and a proper regard to the replacement of the natural resources we employ.

As a publisher, we use a lot of wood pulp to make high-quality paper for printing, and that wood commonly comes from spruce trees. We are therefore currently growing more than 750,000 trees in three Scottish forest plantations: Berrymoss (130 hectares/320 acres), West Touxhill (125 hectares/305 acres) and Deveron Forest (75 hectares/185 acres). The forests we manage contain more than 3.5 times the number of trees employed each year in making paper for the books we manufacture.

Because of this ongoing ecological investment programme, you, as our customer, can have the pleasure and reassurance of knowing that a tree is being cultivated on your behalf to naturally replace the materials used to make the book you are holding.

Our forestry programme is run in accordance with the UK Woodland Assurance Scheme (UKWAS) and will be certified by the internationally recognized Forest Stewardship Council (FSC). The FSC is a non-government organization dedicated to promoting responsible management of the world's forests. Certification ensures forests are managed in an environmentally sustainable and socially responsible way. For further information about this scheme, go to www.annesspublishing.com/trees

Previously published as part of a larger volume, *The Complete Practical Guide to Scrapbooking*.

Publisher's Note:
Although the advice and information in this book are believed to be accurate and true at the
time of going to press, neither the authors nor the publisher can accept any legal responsibility
or liability for any errors or omissions that may be made.

CONTENTS

INTRODUCTION

In the early days of photography, having a picture taken was a notable event. It generally involved a visit to a professional photographer's studio, and the resulting prints – though they might be small and hard to see in tones of sepia or grey – were treasured and displayed in silver frames or ornate albums. Now we live in an age where photography is all around us. It is easier than ever before to take beautiful, detailed, interesting photographs whenever we want, and yet many good prints languish in boxes or drawers. The burgeoning craft of scrapbooking is all about displaying them as they deserve to be seen. But scrapbooks are more than just photograph albums: on their pages you can present your favourite pictures in beautiful, creative settings, accompanied by all the details you need to keep your memories of special times alive and fresh, to enjoy now and to pass down to future generations.

This practical book is full of inspirational and varied scrapbooking ideas. The 65 step-by-step projects use all the basic scrapbooking techniques, from mounting and editing photographs to creating

▼ *Christmas is a good subject for scrapbooks and there is always plenty of decorative material to hand.*

▲ *Old black-and-white photographs used in combination with today's colour prints create interesting style juxtapositions.*

backgrounds and making decorations. The projects are grouped around popular themes such as Children, Weddings, Travel and Family History, to help you decide how to organize your own collections.

Before you begin work on your first page, you need to decide on the size of the album you will use, as this will dictate the size of the layout. Most of the projects in this book are based on 30cm/12in square pages, on which there is plenty of space to mount a good selection of pictures and embellish them creatively. Scrapbooking suppliers offer a huge range of paper, card and other materials in this popular size. Alternatively, you could go for the slightly smaller 21 x 28cm/8½ x 11in. This has the advantage that you can print material on A4 paper to fit it, but it can be more difficult to arrange all the items you want on a single page or double-page spread. Smaller size albums are also available, such as 20cm/8in square, and can be useful if you want to create mini-albums as gifts. Of course, you can also make your own albums and covers in any size you wish, and there are some great ideas in this book for displaying your designs in one-off albums and other unusual ways.

Albums use a number of different binding systems: with three-ring bindings it is easy to move pages around, but they hold a limited number of pages, and the rings make it difficult to display double-page layouts effectively. This is not a problem with post-bound or strap-bound albums, which can expand to take more pages as your collection grows. Whatever you choose, always look for albums and papers that are of "archival" quality, made with acid-free and lignin-free materials, so that your precious prints don't deteriorate once they are mounted.

Like many other aspects of life, the digital revolution plays a vital part in many areas of scrapbooking. Digital cameras and image-editing software have opened up all kinds of photographic possibilities. With no need to buy film, you can take as many experimental pictures as you like and play around with novel formats, colour and special

▼ *Photographs of a family trip to the seaside take on a nostalgic appearance when embellished with 1950s memorabilia.*

▲ *Children are a perennially popular subject for scrapbooks, and children will love looking at their own photographs.*

effects. An internet connection gives you immediate access to online craft suppliers, sources of templates and fonts, and special interest groups with whom you can discuss your projects and display your favourites in virtual galleries. There is now a growing trend towards computer-based scrapbooking, in which stickers, borders and charms are replaced by digital versions which are entirely assembled and displayed on screen.

However, it's certainly not necessary to have a computer in order to enjoy scrapbooking to the full. This craft's great attraction derives from the fact that it is a wonderfully back-to-basics pastime. Good layouts combine artistic flair with genuine hands-on skills with paper, card, fabrics and natural materials. Like the quilting and knitting bees of previous generations, communal scrapbooking events (known as "crops") are strengthening social networks everywhere. As you trim, glue and assemble the elements of your pages, you can rediscover all the enthusiasm and satisfaction you felt when compiling a scrapbook as a child, in the knowledge that you are safeguarding and enhancing your treasured family memorabilia for your own children and for future generations.

Display and presentation

As well as making album pages for your scrapbook, you can also use your presentation skills to mount photographs and other family memorabilia for decorating album covers, memory boxes, memory quilts and even three-dimensional displays.

Archive albums in various formats and bindings are available from scrapbooking stores and other craft suppliers, but you can also buy all the fittings and materials you need to make your own. These unusual formats make particularly attractive gifts commemorating special occasions such as a wedding or the arrival of a baby.

ALBUM COVERS

Designing a special cover for each album gives you a wonderful opportunity to establish its theme and character, so that everyone who sees it will want to look inside and will know instantly what the subject of the chosen album is.

Baby girl album cover

This charming project provides an ideal way to display your favourite baby pictures, and the album will become a family heirloom to be treasured. Make one for each new child in the family, or give them as presents to parents or doting grandparents.

materials and equipment

- metal ruler
- craft knife
- cutting mat
- self-adhesive mount board
- pencil
- polyester wadding (batting), 35 × 33cm/14 × 13in
- scissors
- two pieces of fabric, 35 × 33cm/14 × 13in
- glue stick
- masking tape
- photograph, 15 × 10cm/ 6 × 4in
- watercolour paper, 3 × 30cm/ 1¼ × 12in
- stickers
- hole punch
- 20 sheets of watercolour paper, 29 × 27cm/11¾ × 10¾in
- ribbon

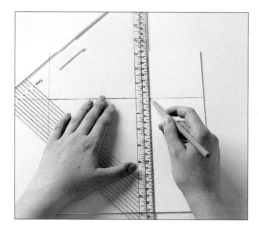

1 Using a metal ruler and craft knife and working on a cutting mat, cut three rectangles each 30 × 28cm/12 × 11¼in and one 30 × 25cm/12 × 10in from self-adhesive mount board. On the smaller rectangle, use a pencil and ruler or set square to draw lines 8cm/3¼in in from each edge to form the aperture for the picture.

2 To make the frame, use a craft knife to cut out the central rectangle and discard. Peel off the protective paper from the adhesive on the mount board and stick the piece of wadding, cut to size, over the frame. Using scissors, trim the wadding to the same size as the mount board.

3 Place one rectangle of fabric right side down and lay the frame over it with the wadding underneath. Fold the surplus fabric to the wrong side of the mount board, mitring the corners carefully. Use a glue stick to secure the raw edges to the frame.

4 Cut two diagonal slits in the centre of the fabric, fold the surplus fabric to the back and glue down. Tape the photograph face down over the aperture so that the picture is visible from the padded fabric side. Cover one of the larger rectangles of mount board with the other piece of fabric.

5 Stick the narrow strip of watercolour paper down one long edge of a second large piece of mount board, then stick the frame in place over the rest of the board. Score along the line where the paper and frame join, so that the cover will open flat. Stick the remaining board to the wrong side of the fabric-covered board to form the back cover.

6 Position a coloured sticker at each corner of the photograph at the front of the album to disguise any raw edges of fabric. For extra security for the stickers, dab a tiny spot of glue from a glue stick on to the fabric as well.

7 Punch two holes centrally at the left edge of the front and back covers and the sheets of watercolour paper; the paper will form the album pages. Position the front and back covers on each side of the pages and lace them together with ribbon.

8 Tie the ribbon ends in a bow. Add a few more stickers above and below the bow along the strip of watercolour paper to complete the cover.

Christmas album cover

A pair of square cake boards in a seasonal design, joined together by simple metal screw posts, form the cover of this festive album. A pair of Scottie dogs, cut from sticky-backed felt, complement the plaid design used here and make a charming motif for the front cover. Use this book when planning your Christmas celebrations: there is plenty of room for guest lists, seating plans, special recipes and gift ideas, and after the festivities you can add Christmas memorabilia such as greetings cards and photos.

materials and equipment

- 2 foil cake boards, 25cm/10in square
- double-sided carpet tape
- scissors
- metallic red corrugated cardboard
- self-adhesive felt in green, black and white
- leather hole punch
- 2 screw posts
- black card (stock)
- pencil
- black cotton tape
- tracing paper
- narrow ribbon
- PVA (white) glue
- self-adhesive black cloth tape
- bradawl (awl)
- 4 split pins

I Place the cake boards side by side, turning them to find the best position to join them (aiming to match the pattern). Stick a 2cm/¾in strip of double-sided carpet tape down each of the edges to be joined.

2 Cut a strip of corrugated cardboard measuring 10 x 25cm/4 x 10in. Stick this over the tape, joining the boards but leaving a 1cm/⅜in gap between them to accommodate the pages.

3 Turn the boards over and cut a rectangle of green self-adhesive felt large enough to cover the inside of the cover. Remove the backing paper and stick in place. Using a leather hole punch, make holes in the top and bottom of the back board, close to the edge of the corrugated cardboard strip. Push a screw post into each hole.

VARIATION: Album cover with a window

Although this album cover has a different subject matter, it is constructed in the same way as the Christmas album cover. The difference is that this album has a window cut in the front, and it has been covered with green felt.

4 From the black card cut 30 sheets 24cm/9½in square and 30 strips 4 × 24cm/ 1½ × 9½in. Make a hole gauge from a spare strip of card and punch out the holes in the card pages and strips. Slip them alternately on to the screw posts.

5 Poke two small holes in the front of the corrugated spine. Thread black tape through the holes and tie in a bow for decoration.

6 Draw a Scottie dog template and use it to cut out a black and a white felt dog. Cross a short length of narrow plaid ribbon at the neck of each dog and glue in position.

7 Remove the backing from each dog. Stick the dogs on to the lower right corner of the front cover, so that the white one slightly overlaps the black one.

8 Cut a rectangle of self-adhesive black felt to make a title plaque. At each corner, push a hole through the cloth, board and green felt using a bradawl. Insert a split pin in each hole and open it up on the inside.

Wedding album cover

The covers of this flamboyant album are made from sturdy silver cake boards, and the front cover is smothered in silk blooms that have been attached to a clear polypropylene sheet. Inside, the album is bound with screw posts, allowing you to add or remove pages as you wish.

1 Using a craft knife and metal ruler on a cutting mat, cut a rectangle of polypropylene measuring 30 x 65cm/12 x 25½in. Score two parallel lines, 5cm/2in apart, across the mid-line, for the spine.

2 Reinforce the spine area on the inside with two lengths of self-adhesive cloth tape, positioning each one centrally over a scored line. Trim the ends flush with the cover.

materials and equipment

- craft knife
- metal ruler
- cutting mat
- polypropylene sheet
- scissors
- self-adhesive cloth tape
- punch
- tack hammer
- assorted silk flowers, large and small
- split pins
- epoxy glue
- 2m/2¼yd wide satin ribbon
- double-sided carpet tape
- 3 silver cake boards, each 30cm/12in square
- weights
- 2 screw posts
- photographic refill pages

3 Using a punch and hammer, make two holes for the screw posts near the top and bottom of the back cover, in the area reinforced by the cloth tape.

4 Arrange the silk flowers on the front cover and mark the position of the centre of each large flower. Cut the bulbous end from the base of each flower using sturdy scissors. Press a split pin through the hole in the centre of each large flower.

5 Using a craft knife, make a small slit at one of the marks on the cover. (Start in the centre and work outwards.) Put your finger firmly on top of the split pin in a large flower and push the ends through the slit.

6 Open the ends of the split pin at the back. Repeat for the other large flowers. Once they are all in place, fill in any gaps by attaching single petals here and there using epoxy glue.

7 Use epoxy glue to attach smaller silk flowers and petals all around the edge of the cover, so that the plastic is completely hidden by them.

8 Cut a length of ribbon long enough to wrap around the book and tie in a bow. Cut another piece to wrap over the spine. With the cover open, lay the longer piece horizontally across the centre of the spine, then wrap the other piece around the spine. Stick both pieces of ribbon in place using double-sided carpet tape.

9 Punch holes in two of the cake boards to correspond with the holes made in the back cover for the screw posts. Sandwich the polypropylene cover, with the horizontal ribbon attached, between the boards, silver side out, and glue all the layers together. Leave the back boards under a weight until the glue is dry. Glue the front cover to the last cake board, with the ribbon sandwiched between and the silver facing out, so that the board forms the inside of the front cover.

10 Position the board so that a narrow silver border is left all around the edge. Leave the glue to harden with the back cover hanging over a table edge and weight the front cover with small weights. Insert the screw posts through the back cover, slip on the photographic refill pages and screw to secure. Tie the ribbon in a decorative bow to close the album.

Patchwork album cover

You do not need to be a skilled stitcher to accomplish a patchwork cover, as the patches are held securely in place with bonding web before sewing. Follow the patchwork pattern known as "Log Cabin" to arrange fabric strips around a central image or position patchwork squares in a random arrangement.

materials and equipment

- small album
- tape measure
- dressmaker's scissors
- extra-heavy non-woven interfacing
- fusible bonding web
- iron
- photograph printed on fabric using image transfer paper
- cotton print fabric in several colours
- pressing cloth
- sewing machine
- sewing thread
- dressmaker's pins

1 Measure the opened book and add 2cm/¾in to the height and 10cm/4in to the width measurements to allow for hems and side flaps. Following these measurements, cut out a piece of extra-heavy non-woven interfacing and a piece of fusible bonding web. Following the manufacturer's instructions, iron the bonding web to the interfacing. Peel off the backing paper.

2 Position your chosen image transfer so that it will appear centrally on the front cover. For the random arrangement, cut small squares of fabric and arrange them around the photo, overlapping them slightly.

3 When you have covered the front and back completely, place a pressing cloth over the patchwork and iron to fuse the scraps to the interfacing.

4 On a sewing machine, topstitch along all the joins between the patches with a satin stitch to cover the raw edges. Overcast around the the outer edges of the cover. With right sides together, turn in 5cm/2in down each short side and pin in place. Stitch along each end of these turnings with a 1cm/⅜in seam to make the side flaps, then turn right side out. Insert the album.

VARIATIONS: Cloth covers and books

For a fabric album cover, measure the opened book and add 2cm/¾in to the height and width measurements for seam allowances. Cut two flaps from contrasting fabric. Turn in and stitch narrow hems on each flap. Decorate the front cover with appliqué and beads, then pin on the flaps, right sides together, stitch with 1cm/⅜in seams and turn.

A cloth book makes a lovely personalized gift album for a baby, and can be filled with familiar images transferred on to fabric. Cut out double pages from sturdy wool fabric or felt and stitch a picture on each page, using images of special people or animals. Add a favourite motif to the front cover and stitch all the layers together at the spine.

ACCORDION ALBUMS

This ingenious and flexible format allows you to protect precious photographs and documents inside an album that closes between hard covers like a book, but can also be fully opened out to make a free-standing display on a table or mantelpiece.

Concertina book

Make this pretty accordion album to hold some of your favourite themed photographs. Choose a selection of luxurious decorative papers in similar shades of mauve for a really striking effect.

materials and equipment

- large rubber stamp in a leaf motif
- metallic ink stamp pad
- translucent paper
- craft knife
- metal ruler
- cutting mat
- thick cardboard
- decorative metallic paper
- glue stick
- bone folder
- handmade paper

1 Stamp the motif on to a selection of papers to choose the effects you like best. To do this, press the stamp into the ink pad to coat the surface with ink, then press the stamp on the paper. Lift it up carefully to avoid smudging. In this case, the motif was stamped on translucent paper using metallic ink. Take care when stamping on to tracing paper, as some stamping inks do not dry well on the resistant surface. If you have difficulty, stamp on a lightweight handmade paper instead. Cut out the motif using a craft knife and metal ruler and working on a cutting mat.

2 To make the front and back covers of the album, cut two pieces of thick cardboard to the required size using a craft knife and metal ruler, and working on a cutting mat. Then cut two pieces of decorative metallic paper 2.5cm/1in larger all round than the cardboard. Lay the paper right side down and glue one piece of cardboard to the centre of each piece. Cut across the corners of the paper, then glue the edges and carefully fold them over to stick them down securely on the cardboard. Turn the front cover over and glue the stamped leaf motif in the centre.

◀**3** Cut a long strip of translucent paper slightly narrower than the height of the cover boards. This will form the folded pages of the album. Measure the width of the album cover and make folds along the strip of paper to match. To do this, carefully and accurately measure the distance from one fold to another; use a metal ruler and bone folder to score and crease the paper to produce a succession of accordion folds. Trim off any excess paper at the end. When you have finished, ensure that the paper folds into a neat pile, and that it fits neatly inside the album.

4 Glue one end of the folded translucent paper on to the front cover of the album, then cover the whole with a sheet of handmade paper to coordinate with the rest of the album. Stick the other end of the translucent paper to the back cover and cover this with a second sheet of handmade paper. Fold up the book and place it under a heavy weight to prevent the papers from buckling as the glue dries.

Accordion wrap

This attractive book uses a folding technique developed in Japan to store long scrolls of paper. The paper used here for the covers contains fragments of coloured silk and threads, added to the paper pulp before forming the sheets.

materials and equipment

- 2 pieces of mounting board, 15 x 20cm/6 x 8in
- glue stick
- 2 sheets of handmade paper, 19 x 24cm/7½ x 9½in
- scissors
- craft knife
- metal ruler
- cutting mat
- narrow satin ribbon
- tapestry needle
- white cartridge (construction) paper 112 x 19cm/44 x 7½in
- bone folder

1 To make the covers, apply glue to one side of each piece of mounting board. Place the board centrally on the wrong side of each piece of handmade paper.

2 Cut diagonally across the corners of the two sheets of paper. Fold the excess paper over the boards and glue in place.

3 Using a craft knife, metal ruler and cutting mat, cut a 1cm/⅜in slit in the centre of each long side on both covers.

4 Cut four 25cm/10in lengths of ribbon. Using a tapestry needle, thread one through each slit and glue the end to the board.

VARIATION: Fan book

Fold a circle of paper into twelfths and cut down one fold to the centre. Trim the edge. Make two covers to fit the shape and glue to the end folds.

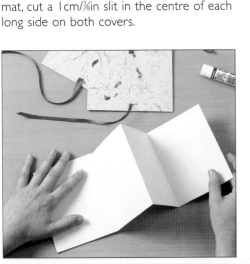

5 Using the bone folder, fold the cartridge paper into accordion pleats to form eight equal sections using accordion pleats.

6 Glue the end sections of the paper to the inside of the covers, positioning them centrally. Make sure the two covers line up.

7 Tie one pair of ribbons to create a book with turning pages.

DISPLAY BOARDS

Rather than keeping all your creative ideas tucked away in albums, it can be fun to make scrapbook-style displays to go on the wall. Old prints fade easily, so it is a good idea to have copies made to use in this way and to keep the originals safely away from the light.

Seaside memory board

This collection of holiday memories serves both as a decorative feature for your wall and as a noticeboard to which other mementoes can be added from time to time. It could even be used as a memo board for day-to-day reminders. While you are on your trip, persuade the whole family to look for pretty souvenirs to remind them of your happy time on the beach together.

materials and equipment

- collection of seaside photographs
- pictures from printed sources of marine subjects such as sea, sand, sky, pebbles and shells
- old maps showing large areas of sea
- natural objects such as feathers and small shells
- scissors
- metal ruler
- craft knife
- cutting mat
- lightweight white board
- textured paper
- spray adhesive
- transparent photo corners

1 Spread out your family photographs, together with printed pictures from other sources, maps and seaside ephemera, to decide which to use. Cut out some of the background material with scissors, tear some pictures to give them ragged edges, and trim others with a metal ruler and craft knife so that you have a range of different textures and edges to the collection.

2 Assemble the larger, more abstract pictures of sky and sea on the board, overlapping them with areas of textured paper to make a background for the photographs. When you are happy with the arrangement, glue the background pictures down securely with spray adhesive. Arrange feathers and other pieces of seaside ephemera on the board.

◄ **3** Complete the memory board by adding your photographs to the arrangement, and secure them using transparent photo corners. If you are using duplicate prints you could stick them in position with glue once you have finalized the composition, but using photo corners enables you to place other mementoes behind the photos as your collection grows. Glue additional pieces of ephemera, such as small shells, around the photographs.

VARIATION: **Seashore album**

For a seaside-themed album, cover the boards with an enlarged detail of a photograph of sand and sea, and glue a real seashell to the front – look for flat shells when you're on the beach.

Pressed flower noticeboard

Natural linen and linen tape tone beautifully with the pressed flowers and leaves and the colour-washed wooden frame in this attractive design.

materials and equipment

- large, flat, rectangular wooden picture frame
- off-white emulsion (latex) paint
- medium-sized decorator's paintbrush
- pressed flowers and leaves
- measuring tape
- PVA (white) glue
- fine artist's paintbrush
- spray matt acrylic varnish
- natural linen or linen-look fabric
- scissors
- sheet of MDF (medium density fibreboard) cut to fit frame
- staple gun
- soft pencil
- linen dressmaking tape
- hammer
- decorative upholstery nails
- picture wire or cord for hanging

1 Paint the picture frame with a coat of off-white emulsion (latex) paint. Apply the paint in a thin wash, so that the texture of the wood shows through. Leave to dry.

2 Arrange the flowers and leaves with the help of a measuring tape. Starting in the centre of one short side of the frame and working outwards, apply a little PVA glue to the back of each flower and stick in place.

3 When the design is complete, leave until the glue is dry then spray the frame with matt acrylic varnish. Repeat if necessary but take care not to flatten the flowers.

4 Cut a piece of linen 5cm/2in larger all round than the MDF. Stretch the fabric over the board and secure it at the back with a staple gun, starting in the centre of each side and folding the corners neatly.

5 On the right side, mark out a large central diamond using a soft pencil. Cut four lengths of linen tape to fit and lay in place, stapling them together at the corners.

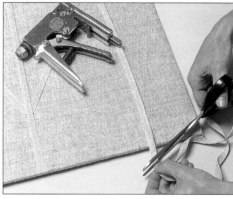

6 Arrange more lines of tape in a pleasing design, weaving them over and under each other. Trim the ends and secure at the back of the board with the staple gun.

7 On the right side, secure the linen tape with upholstery nails spaced at regular intervals. Fit the decorated board into the frame and attach picture wire or cord.

HERITAGE QUILTS

Traditional quilts have often been used to record special events or memories by applying embroidery or incorporating symbolic patchwork shapes. With the latest range of transfer papers you can now create a photographic quilt made up of family pictures for posterity too.

Memory quilt

This beautiful album quilt was made to commemorate the 70th birthday of the maker's mother. Some of the ivory silk fabric used was taken from a wedding dress, giving it particular sentimental value.

materials and equipment

- black and white photographs
- scraps of ivory silk in a variety of textures and shades
- image transfer paper
- iron
- paper
- pencil
- dressmaker's scissors
- calico
- measuring tape
- dressmaker's pins
- sewing machine
- ivory sewing thread
- ivory silk for the quilt backing
- quilt interlining
- tacking thread and needle
- coffee silk for binding the edges
- metallic sewing thread

1 Transfer the photographs on to silk, using a transfer paper suitable for the fabric. Decide on the finished block size and estimate how many blocks you will need to make by working out a plan on paper. Cut the block squares from calico, adding a seam allowance all around of 2cm/¾in. Trim each transferred photograph and pin to the block through the border to avoid damaging the prints.

2 Cut random strips of different silks. Pin one strip right side down to one side of the photograph. Stitch the strip down, making sure the seam does not obscure the image, then flip the strip over to conceal the stitching and press lightly. Add the next strip at an angle, covering the end of the previous strip. Repeat, working clockwise round the image, and cut away excess fabric from each strip before adding the next.

3 Complete each calico block in the same way, mixing the colours and textures of silk randomly. When you have added all the strips, press each patch then trim away the excess fabric with scissors, leaving a 2cm/¾in seam allowance around the block.

4 Pin and stitch the blocks together in rows, adding extra strips of silk between them. Join the rows, then add a border. To assemble the quilt, place the backing right side down and the interlining on top. Finally place the quilt top right side up on top. Tack (baste) all three layers together.

5 Decorate the quilt with machine or hand quilting before binding the edges with coffee silk. Finish the design with machine embroidery using metallic thread in a zig-zag or other embroidery stitch.

Paper quilt wallhanging

In this exciting and original hanging, the images are not just framed but actually become part of the vibrantly coloured handmade paper squares. Paper pulp and pigments for dyeing it can be bought from craft suppliers.

materials and equipment

- collection of photographs or other souvenirs such as tickets, labels or press cuttings
- aluminium mesh
- strong scissors
- 2.5cm/1in-wide masking tape
- absorbent non-woven kitchen cloths
- recycled paper pulp
- paper dyes in 2–3 colours
- 2–3 large plastic bowls
- paper string or embroidery thread (floss)
- 60cm/24in dowelling, 6mm/¼in diameter

1 With your collection of materials in front of you, decide on a standard size for each patch and the number of patches that are required to make the hanging. In this case each patch will be 15cm/6in square.

2 To make the moulds for the paper, cut a 17.5cm/7in square of aluminium mesh, and a strip 15 x 4cm/6 x 1½in. Fold strips of masking tape over each edge of the mesh shapes to cover the sharp edges.

3 Cover a large board with several layers of non-woven kitchen cloth. Dye two or three batches of pulp following the manufacturer's instructions. Immerse the square mesh in the background colour pulp and lift the first square out of the bowl.

4 Turn the mesh carefully to deposit the square in the top corner of the couching cloth. Repeat to make a total of nine squares, laying them in three rows of three. Use the masking tape binding as a guide for the spacing between the squares.

5 Cut 36 lengths of paper string or embroidery thread 10cm/4in long, and lay them over the spaces to join the squares. Cut nine lengths 9cm/3½in long to make the hanging loops. Double these and arrange them along one side.

6 Couch nine more squares of the same coloured pulp on top of the first set, to hold the strings or threads in place.

7 Arrange your collection of images centrally on the squares of wet pulp.

8 Using different coloured pulp and the smaller mould, couch strips of pulp over the edges of the images to hold them in place. Leave for several days to dry naturally, then thread the dowelling rod through the loops.

KEEPSAKE BOXES

For small collections, or treasured three-dimensional objects that cannot be fitted into an album, a keepsake box is the answer. Look out for good quality packaging that can be recycled, or buy plain cardboard boxes from craft stores and decorate them to match the subject of your collection.

Découpage memory box

The art of decorating with paper scraps, which are overlaid and varnished to give the appearance of a hand-painted finish is known as découpage. This box is prettily decorated with pictures of coloured feathers, cats, flowers and fans, and finished with a pink ribbon border – every girl's ideal treasure box.

materials and equipment

- plain hexagonal cardboard box with lid
- acrylic or household emulsion (latex) paint in eau de Nil
- paintbrush
- scraps of old manuscript paper, or new paper aged by dyeing in tea
- glue stick
- selection of cut-out paper scraps printed with images of cats, fans, feathers and flowers
- acrylic matt varnish
- measuring tape
- scissors
- fabric ribbon
- fabric glue
- assorted buttons
- needle and thread

1 Paint the box inside and out with two coats of eau de Nil paint and leave to dry. Tear the manuscript paper into scraps and glue these to the sides and lid of the box. Cover with the printed scraps, overlapping them as desired. Apply two to three coats of acrylic varnish, leaving each coat to dry.

2 Measure the rim of the lid and cut a length of ribbon to this measurement. Using fabric glue, stick the ribbon around the rim. Using the same glue, stick a selection of buttons in assorted designs around the rim, on top of the ribbon.

3 Make a simple rosette shape with another length of ribbon and secure by stitching through the central folds. Stitch a button in to the centre, then glue the rosette to the centre of the box lid.

VARIATION: Travel memory box

To house a collection of holiday souvenirs, cover a travel-themed memory box with découpage using scraps of maps featuring appropriate destinations.

Fabric-covered box

Covering a box with a luxurious fabric such as linen, velvet or silk makes a very special setting for small treasures such as a collection of love letters and romantic trinkets. This box is cleverly constructed with ribbon ties so that it lies flat before assembly and could make a lovely surprise gift. If you are making the box as a memento of a family wedding you may even be able to obtain a little spare wedding dress fabric to make an extra-special reminder of the occasion for the bride.

materials and equipment

- craft knife
- metal ruler
- cutting mat
- strong cardboard
- squared pattern paper
- pencil
- scissors
- dressmaker's pins
- pale lilac linen
- dressmaker's scissors
- tacking (basting) thread
- needle
- narrow velvet ribbon
- grosgrain ribbon
- Ric-rac braid
- sewing machine
- sewing thread
- iron
- small embroidered motif
- fabric glue

1 Using a craft knife and metal ruler and working on a cutting mat, from strong cardboard cut out a base and a lid, each 19 x 15cm/7½ x 6in; two long sides each 19 x 7.5cm/7½ x 3in; and two short sides each 15 x 7.5cm/6 x 3in. These will be slipped inside the cover to make the box rigid.

2 Make a paper pattern using the measurements on the template at the back of the book as a guide. Add a 1.5cm/⅝in seam allowance all around the pattern. Pin the pattern to a piece of lilac linen folded in half along the grain and cut out two matching pieces of fabric.

3 Using a contrasting coloured thread, and working on the piece of fabric intended for the right side of the cover, tack (baste) the fabric to mark out the stitching lines for the different sections of the box, following the guides on the template. Cut eight 15cm/6in lengths of narrow velvet ribbon for the corner ties and two 30cm/12in lengths of grosgrain ribbon for the front ties.

VARIATIONS: More fabric ideas

To memorialize a beloved pet, cover a box with fabric on to which you have transferred a favourite photograph.

Cover an old shoe box with decorative papers or fabrics appropriate for the occasion and add ribbons.

4 On the right side of the fabric, pin and tack a length of Ric-rac braid along the seam line around three sides of the box lid. Pin the ties in place at the corners and pin one piece of grosgrain ribbon to the lid.

5 Pin the last piece of grosgrain ribbon to the centre front section of the box base. Stitch the ribbon ties down with a straight machine stitch, turning the raw edges underneath to neaten.

6 Pin the two pieces of fabric right sides together and stitch all around the edges of the box. Leave the long side at the front of the base open so that the cardboard sections can be slipped inside the cover. Clip the corners and trim the seam allowance, then turn the cover through to the right side and press.

7 Push the first piece of cardboard for the lid through the opening along the long side. Neatly stitch along the lid edge to enclose it using a zipper foot on the machine. Insert the cardboard for the long side at the back and enclose with another line of stitches, followed by the pieces for the short sides and the large piece for the base. Enclose each piece of cardboard with a line of stitches. Finally, insert the last piece for the long side at the front of the box.

8 When all the cardboard is in place, turn in the seam allowance of the opening and neatly slipstitch the seam. Glue an embroidered motif on to the box lid with fabric glue. Then tie the ribbon ties at each corner to assemble the box.

Butterfly photograph

These two charming ideas for presenting a single photograph use matching butterfly motifs, which are folded and glued so that they appear to flutter around the picture. Punched holes give their wings a lacy appearance.

materials and equipment

- pencil
- paper
- scissors
- selection of pastel-coloured papers, including white
- cutting mat
- craft knife
- revolving leather punch
- fancy-edged scissors
- fine corrugated white cardboard
- glue stick
- heavy white paper
- coloured card (stock)
- photographs
- transparent photo corners

1 Enlarge the butterfly template at the back of the book in three different sizes and cut them out. Place a template on a piece of folded coloured paper and trace around it. Cut out the small angled shapes in the wings using a craft knife and working on a cutting mat, and make decorative round holes in various sizes using a leather punch.

2 Keeping the paper folded, cut round the outline of the butterfly with fancy-edged scissors. Make a selection of butterfly motifs in different sizes and colours. Do not flatten out the central folds. To make winged cards, cut out one wing only, then cut out a rectangle around the wing using fancy-edged scissors. Fold the wing outwards.

3 To make a foundation on which to mount the butterflies, enlarge the frame template so that it is about 2.5cm/1in larger all round than the photograph, then cut it out. Position it on a piece of white corrugated cardboard and draw round it lightly with a pencil. Cut out the shape, taking care not to crush the ridges of the cardboard. Glue the cut-out on to a slightly larger rectangle of heavy white paper and mount this on a larger piece of coloured card.

VARIATION: Butterfly theme

Butterflies are a perennially popular motif. They can be stencilled, stamped, cut out from paper and applied in different ways to album pages.

4 Carefully make four tiny marks at the corners where you intend to mount the photograph, then arrange the butterfly motifs around the frame, slotting some individual butterflies inside the winged cards. Glue them in place using a glue stick. Finally, attach the photograph to the mount using transparent photo corners.

5 To make the photo mailer, cut a long strip of heavy white paper slightly wider than the photograph and long enough to enclose it plus an overlap for the butterfly. Crease the vertical folds. Cut out one small and one large butterfly motif from coloured paper, then cut out a half large motif from the end flap. Using the photo as a guide, position and cut four diagonal slots to take the corners.

6 Assemble the photo mailer by sticking the large butterfly to the front of the card in such a position that the wings slot through the folded half motif cut in the flap. The action of slotting the wings together will keep the card closed. Stick a small motif on the front of the card and mount the photograph inside.

Children

Babies and children are of course among the most popular subjects for scrapbooking: all parents long to preserve their memories of their offspring as they grow up so quickly. For most people, it's also when they have their own children that they become most aware of the need to pass on the family history to future generations. There is nothing older children like more than revisiting their own earliest memories – seeing pictures of their former little selves and being reminded of special times they can just remember, or discovering what they were like as babies, before their memories begin. As well as photographs, of which you will have plenty to choose from, include some of the children's early works of art or attempts at writing.

Album page for a baby boy

Soft pastel shades dictate the look of this album page, which has a contemporary style. Keep a tiny but important memento, such as the baby's hospital identification tag, safely inside a small clear plastic envelope.

1 Cut out rectangles of plain and printed paper, and arrange them on the heavy white paper. Use different-sized rectangles to make a pleasing layout. Glue in position. Arrange the collage items on the background. Small mementoes can be placed in clear plastic envelopes. Glue all the background items in place.

2 Take a small piece of white card and draw a simple motif, such as a toy boat, on the wrong side of it. Working on a cork mat or corrugated cardboard to protect the work surface, use a bodkin or paper piercer to make pinpricks at regular intervals along the outline of the design using the pencil line as a guide.

materials and equipment

- scissors
- plain paper in pastel colours
- striped printed paper
- heavy white paper
- glue stick
- baby mementoes
- small, clear plastic envelope
- white card (stock)
- pencil
- cork mat or corrugated cardboard
- bodkin or paper piercer
- fancy-edged scissors in wavy and postage stamp designs
- rotating leather hole punch
- lettering stencil
- craft knife
- cutting mat
- baby Ric-rac braid

3 Cut out a rectangle of blue paper using wavy-edged scissors. Then cut out the pinpricked motif with fancy-edged scissors in a postage stamp design and glue it on the blue paper.

VARIATION: A patchwork background

Simple photographs can be enhanced in many ways. Here a single photograph takes centre stage and the ephemera that is added is colour co-ordinated to hold the design idea together. The stripey pastel patchwork background is appropriately coloured for a baby boy and matches his clothing.

The zipper pocket at the bottom of the page is a good place to keep any small items of memorabilia, such as small cards expressing good wishes from friends and family. The cute faces are a fun addition to this light-hearted album page.

4 Make a mount for the photograph by cutting out a piece of white card larger all round than the photograph, using wavy-edged scissors. Pierce small decorative holes all around the edges of the card using a rotating leather hole punch.

5 Place a lettering stencil over a rectangular piece of blue paper and stencil the letter of your choice on the card. Cut the letter out carefully with a craft knife, working on a cutting mat. Trim the corners of the paper shape with scissors to round them gently.

6 Mount the cut-out letter on a rectangle of pale yellow paper, then on a larger fancy-edged rectangle of white card. Pierce a small hole in the centre top of the label and thread it with a short length of baby Ric-rac braid. Tie this in a bow. Carefully glue everything to the background.

Album page for a baby girl

Pages dedicated to baby girls don't always have to be pale pink and frilly. This cheeky picture called for a bolder treatment, so the page uses bright colours and a stitched paisley motif with the sparkle of tiny gems.

materials and equipment

- scraps of card (card stock)
- pencil
- felt squares in blue, lime green, light purple and dark purple
- scissors
- stranded embroidery thread (floss) in lime green, fuchsia and turquoise
- needle
- small self-adhesive gems
- tweezers
- 30cm/12in square sheet of bright pink card (card stock)
- glue stick
- small buckle
- self-adhesive foam pads
- photograph
- chipboard letters
- craft paint in purple
- artist's brush

1 Draw three large and two small paisley shapes on card and cut them out. Use them as templates to cut out five felt shapes in assorted colours.

2 Work a row of backstitch around the edge of each felt shape using six strands of contrasting embroidery thread. Work three lazy daisy stitches in the centre of each large shape and one on each small shape.

3 Stick a small self-adhesive gem to the embroidery stitches in the centre of each paisley shape, grasping the gems with tweezers to make this easier.

4 Cut a strip of purple felt 2cm/¾in wide and 30cm/12in long and glue it down the left side of the background card near the edge. Decorate a small buckle with more sticky gems and glue it to the felt belt.

5 Glue the decorated felt shapes to the matching card shapes. Stick two foam pads on the back of each small paisley shape so that they will be slightly raised.

6 Position the photograph centrally in the area to the right of the felt strip and glue it to the background. Arrange the three large paisley shapes down the left side of the picture, then position the small shapes between them. Glue all the shapes in place.

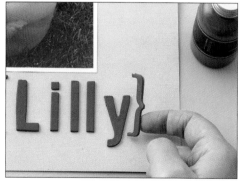

7 Paint chipboard letters to spell the child's name in purple to match the felt shapes and leave to dry. Glue them in place at the bottom right of the layout.

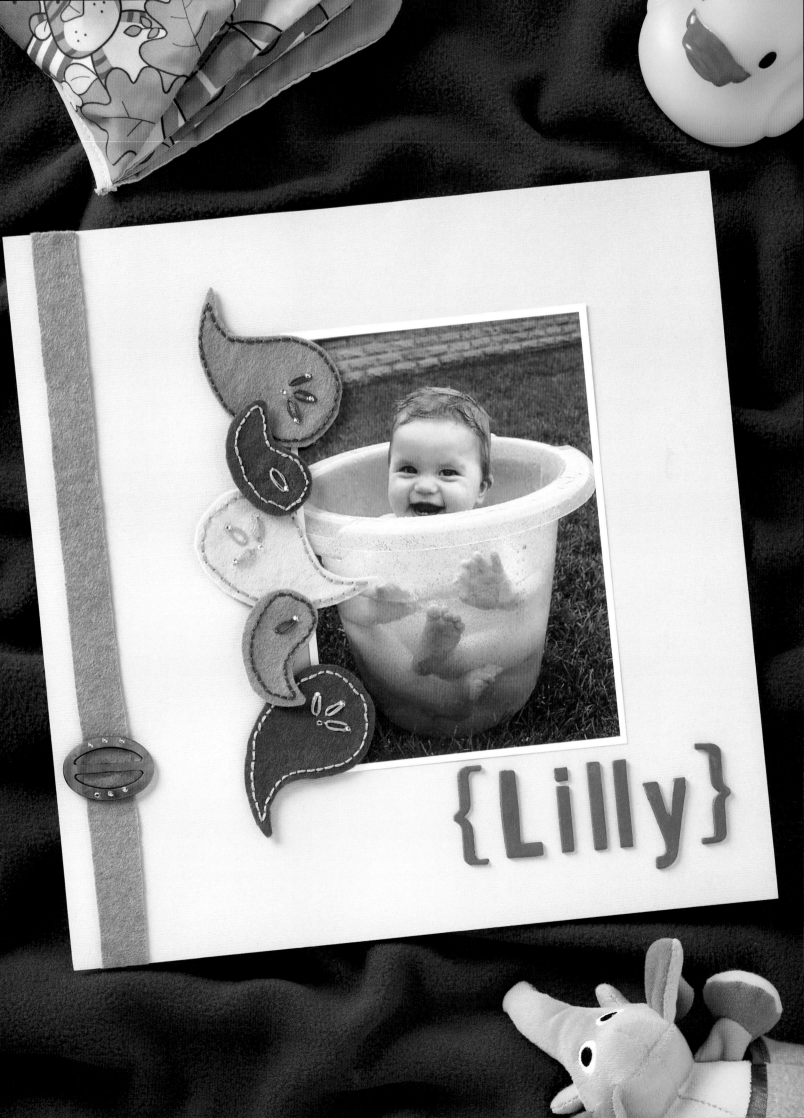

{Lilly}

Schoolday memories

This memento of your schooldays will bring back memories of past escapades, glories and disasters. Indulge yourself and relive all those carefree times by making a schooldays album page.

materials and equipment

- brick-effect dolls' house paper
- sharp scissors
- glue stick
- envelope
- selection of school photographs
- transparent photo corners
- small labels
- black pen
- striped grosgrain ribbon
- metal badge
- embroidered pocket and cap badges
- school reports
- star stickers

1 Cut two sheets of brick-effect paper to match the size of your album pages and glue in position. Glue the envelope in one corner so that the flap faces upwards. Arrange the photographs on the page then secure with photo corners.

2 Next to each photograph, stick a handwritten label giving the year each picture was taken (or use computer-printed labels if you prefer). The album pages here show four generations of schoolchildren.

Starting school is a major milestone for every child, but after just a few weeks they all seem to settle into their new life, making friends, learning new skills and starting on the path to independence. Mark the progress from the first uncertain day to being one of a trio of best friends with a special album page.

materials and equipment

- 30cm/12in square sheet of plain background paper
- brick-effect paper
- two or more photographs
- photo corners
- small labels
- alphabet fridge magnets
- photocopier
- scissors
- coloured pencils

3 Fold the grosgrain ribbon in half and attach the metal badge to the top of the ribbon near the fold. Trim the ribbon ends to create a V shape. Glue the ribbon to the flap of the envelope. (Always keep a sheet of paper between the two album pages when they are closed to prevent the badge damaging the pictures.)

1 Cut two 2.5cm/1in strips of brick-effect paper and stick them along the top and bottom of the background paper. Mount the photographs in the centre with photo corners. Add a printed or handwritten date label under each.

2 Photocopy the fridge magnets and the pencils, reducing the size as necessary. Cut them out individually and arrange around the pictures. The letters can spell out a caption or be placed randomly. Glue everything in place.

4 Glue the embroidered badges to the pages, positioning the cap badge just above the envelope. Fill the envelope with extra pictures and school reports. Finally, arrange a sprinkling of star stickers over the pages.

Polka-dot mini-album

This handy-sized accordion album, in its own brightly decorated matching box, could be filled with a selection of photographs from every stage of a child's life, to make an enchanting gift for a proud grandparent.

materials and equipment

- rectangular cardboard box
- handmade paper in orange, pink, turquoise and green
- small coins
- pencil
- scissors
- hole punch
- glue stick
- thick card (stock)
- metal ruler
- craft knife and cutting mat
- paper parcel tape
- thin green card
- pair of compasses
- thin satin ribbon

1 Cover the box with orange handmade paper. Draw around small coins on to orange, pink, turquoise and green paper. Cut out all the circles. Punch small holes in the centre of some circles using a hole punch. Glue the circles to the top and sides of the box, overlapping some of them.

2 Measure and mark out four identical rectangles of thick card to a size that will fit neatly inside the box. Cut them out using a craft knife and a metal ruler and working on a cutting mat.

3 Place the rectangles side by side in a row, leaving gaps of about 3mm/⅛in between them. Cut six strips of paper tape, slightly longer than the card. Stick the tape to the cards, over the gaps, to join them together. Repeat on the other side. Leave to dry, then trim away the excess tape.

4 Fold along the joins to make an accordion album. Cut eight pieces of turquoise handmade paper to the same dimensions as the cards. Glue one piece to the front and one to the back of each page of the album.

5 Cut six strips of orange paper 2.5cm/1in wide to match the height of the pages. Glue a strip over the middle of each fold on the front and back.

6 Decorate the front of the album with small multicoloured circles of paper to match the box.

7 Draw a circle 6cm/2¼in in diameter on thin green card and cut it out. Trim a small photo into a slightly smaller circle and glue it to the green circle to make a tag.

8 Punch a hole in the top of the tag and add a length of thin satin ribbon as a tie. Fill the album with photographs. Tie the tag around the album to keep it closed, then place the album in the box.

VARIATION: Snow scene

Children playing in the snow are always full of fun and vitality, with bright smiles and rosy cheeks. Once the snow stops falling and the sun comes out, it's a great time to take photographs of them for your album, to store up memories of exciting days.

On this scrapbook page, blue and white spotted paper has been used to resemble a snowy sky, and the torn white edges and glittering stars, plus the pale colouring of all the elements, help to reinforce the cold, bright winter light in the photograph. You could create a similar snowy background for a winter page by sticking on individual self-adhesive dots in a random arrangement on plain paper.

Growing up together

Birthdays, Christmas and Easter holidays are family times that are especially important to grandparents, aunts, uncles and cousins. Keep a record of how the children are growing in the intervening months by collecting together pictures taken on these special occasions.

materials and equipment

- six photographs
- coloured paper
- corner punch
- 30cm/12in square of background paper
- tear-off calendar
- glue stick

1 Trim all the photographs to measure 7 × 9cm/2¾ × 3½in. Glue each on to a piece of coloured paper and trim the margins to 1cm/⅜in all around.

2 Trim the corners with a decorative punch to give the frames a pretty, lacy look.

VARIATION: Family secrets

Here's another idea for a family album page that shows all the children together yet allows each of them to make a personal contribution – if you can persuade them to take part.

Create matching mini-folders from thin card (stock), one for each child, and decorate the fronts with small photographs, each mounted on a torn square of handmade floral paper. Fasten each folder with a short loop of ribbon and a small button.

Inside the little folders you could insert a few folded pages of white paper and get each child to write something about themselves and what they have been doing, or make up a story or a poem, or draw some pictures. Alternatively, you could paste in more photographs or other memorabilia, or write your own account of your children's progress and achievements. Decorate the rest of the page with a few small embellishments and give it a title and a date.

You could make a page of this kind every year as an ongoing record of your growing offspring, with pictures shot specially for the album page. Both you and other family members, and the children themselves, will enjoy looking back over the years to see these snapshots of themselves as developing individuals within a family group.

3 Arrange the pictures in two scattered rows of three, in chronological order, on the background paper.

4 Add a few tear-off pages from the calendar, scattered over the page. Circle the dates when the pictures were taken on the calendar pages.

Special occasions

Many of our most memorable and enjoyable experiences occur on the important annual festivals such as Christmas, Easter and Thanksgiving, which give a regular rhythm to family life and are traditionally times when everyone wants to get together with relatives and friends for informal and joyful celebrations.

As well as these parties, there are the very special occasions that mark life's milestones, such as graduation, engagement, marriage and the birth of a baby, to name but a few. All these high days and holidays demand to be commemorated by special pages in your albums, and all make great themes for which a wealth of decorative material is available, as well as a good collection of photographs of the event. The following pages include ideas for pages based on both seasonal festivities and more personal celebrations.

Valentine's celebration

The traditional imagery of Valentine's Day is perfect for an album page expressing the way you feel about your partner. Use the phrases on this layout as inspiration for your own special messages to the one you love.

1 Cut a 12 × 4in/30 × 10cm rectangle of pearl white paper and glue it to the left-hand side of the red card background, aligning the edges, to make a wide border.

2 Print out all the words and phrases, except "Forever", on to white paper. Trim "I love you because…" and "…you're wonderful!" to thin white strips measuring 10 × 2cm/4 × ¾in. Glue to the top and bottom of the border.

3 Glue two swing tags on to the back of a sheet of silver paper, and one on to red paper. Cut the papers to shape by cutting around the edges of the tags. Re-punch the holes with an eyelet punch.

4 Cut out the three printed phrases and glue one to the front of each tag. Punch three small hearts from red vellum and glue these to the tags, over the text.

5 Position the tags on the border. Mark the positions of the holes for the elastic at the sides of the tags and punch the holes with an eyelet punch. Thread the elastic to make crosses and tie at the back. Insert the tags with the red tag in the centre.

6 To make the frame, draw a 12.5 × 15cm/ 5 × 6in rectangle on thick card. Draw a second rectangle inside it, 2cm/¾in smaller all round. Cut it out using a craft knife and metal ruler. Dry-brush a thin coat of parchment-coloured paint over the frame and leave it to dry.

7 Cut out four small discs of white card. Inscribe the letters L, O, V and E on the discs using rub-on letters.

8 Punch a small hole in the top of each disc using an eyelet punch. Insert an eyelet into each, then a length of ribbon. Glue the four discs to the top of the page.

9 Cut out the printed words "you" and "me". Glue them to small heart-shaped tags. Attach the hearts to the page beside the border panel using white eyelets.

materials and equipment

- scissors
- pearl white paper
- metal ruler
- pencil
- craft knife
- cutting mat
- 30cm/12in square sheet of thin red card (stock)
- spray adhesive
- computer and printer
- thin white paper
- 3 small swing tags
- silver and red paper
- small eyelet punch
- tack hammer
- red vellum paper
- heart punch
- thin round elastic in silver
- thick card (stock)
- acrylic paint in parchment
- paintbrush
- white card
- gold rub-on letters
- 6 eyelets
- thin red and silver ribbon
- 2 small heart tags
- white vellum
- thin steel wire
- strong clear glue
- photograph
- masking tape
- 4 photo corners

10 Print the word "Forever" on to a sheet of white vellum. Trim closely, then glue with spray adhesive to a larger strip of white vellum. Attach the strip to the bottom of the page.

11 Cut two pieces of steel wire 15cm/6in long. Bend into two hearts. Twist the ends of one heart together and loop the second heart through the first before twisting the ends. Glue the entwined hearts over the vellum panel using strong clear glue.

12 Attach the photo to the back of the painted frame with strips of masking tape. Position the framed picture in the centre of the red area of the page and attach it using photo corners.

An engagement

This simple and beautiful layout expresses a single idea very clearly: the love and happiness of the newly engaged couple. The use of translucent vellum for the heart shapes creates a pretty, layered look. It's essential to use spray adhesive for the vellum, as any other glue will show through.

materials and equipment

- polka-dot paper
- metal ruler
- pencil
- craft knife
- cutting mat
- 30cm/12in square sheet of thin cream card (card stock)
- spray adhesive
- gold paper
- scallop-edged scissors
- red vellum
- light pink vellum
- dark pink paper
- 1 large photograph and 3 small ones

1 Cut a 30 x 18cm/12 x 7in rectangle of polka-dot paper using a craft knife and metal ruler and working on a cutting mat. Glue the paper to the right-hand side of the cream card, aligning the outer edges.

2 Cut three rectangles of gold paper 7 x 5cm/2¾ x 2in, and one 17 x 14.5cm/6¾ x 5¾in. Trim all the sides with scallop-edged scissors. Cut out the centres to make frames with narrow borders.

3 Glue the large frame to the lower part of the polka dot paper. Trace the heart templates at the back of the book. Cut out one large heart and one small heart from light pink vellum, and one medium heart and one small heart each from red vellum and dark pink paper. Glue the small hearts down the left-hand side and the medium hearts to the right above the large frame.

4 Glue the large pink heart to the middle of the page. Glue the small frames over the small hearts and glue the photographs in position in the frames.

VARIATION: Other special occasions

Right: This mosaic treatment is a good way to include plenty of individual shots of people who attend a farewell party. The scrapbook album page is a perfect record of those who attended as well as a good reminder of the occasion.

Far right: To mark the occasion of being voted lord mayor, this scrapbook album page is decorated with appropriately sombre colours.

Below: A handmade album cover for a special wedding anniversary is decorated with a ribbon of satin roses. The matt cream textured boards are appropriate for the subject.

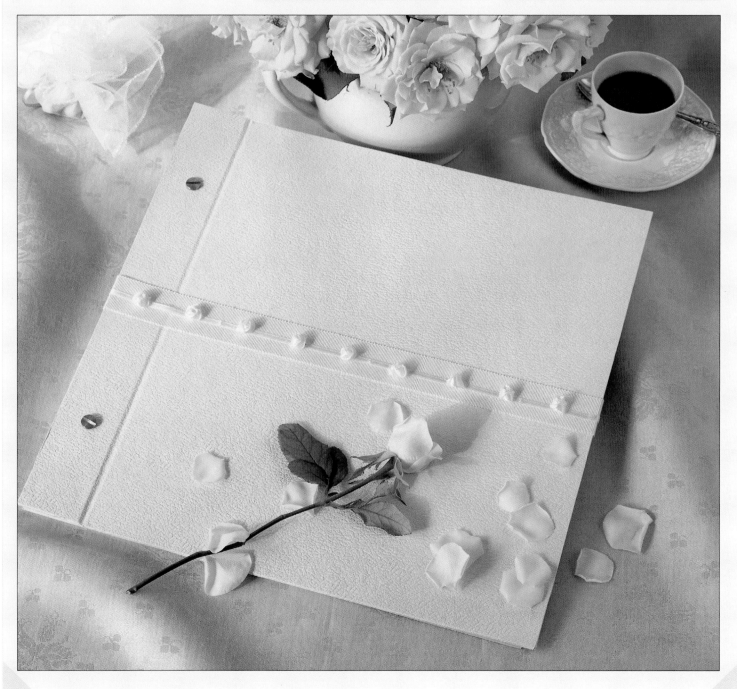

Christmas celebration

It's a treat to use the traditional festive colours of green and red for a Christmas layout, and deep red velvet-effect paper creates a fabulous rich background. Add plenty of gold and glitter for a thoroughly opulent look.

materials and equipment

- red velvet-effect paper
- ruler
- pencil
- scissors
- spray adhesive
- 30cm/12in square sheet of green card (stock)
- tartan border sticker
- sheet of gold glitter card (stock)
- Christmas photograph
- fancy-edged scissors
- glue dots
- star punch
- oval cutter
- gold paper ribbon

1 Cut a rectangle measuring 28 × 22.5cm/ 11 × 9in from the red velvet-effect paper and glue it to the green card, leaving a narrow border of green at the top, bottom and right-hand side.

2 Use a tartan border sticker to decorate the left-hand edge of the red velvet paper, sticking it centrally along the join.

VARIATION: Digital Christmas

Online scrapbooking stores offer a host of backgrounds and other ingredients for seasonally themed digital pages, so it's very easy to put together a page including pictures of your Christmas festivities. You could even add pictures of the children opening their presents and email it to friends and family on the big day itself.

3 Cut a piece of gold glitter card slightly larger all around than the photograph. Trim the edge using fancy-edged scissors. Glue the photograph to the gold card then glue in place on the background.

4 Using the tree template at the back of the book cut a Christmas tree out of green card. Punch some stars from gold card and glue in place. Glue the tree to the background. Cut three gold oval baubles and punch a hole near one end of each for threading a short length of paper ribbon through. Glue all the decorations in place.

Thanksgiving

A collection of vintage scraps and a row of patches cut from homespun fabrics embody the traditional values of American Thanksgiving celebrations, suggesting comfort and warmth. A brown paper background and manila photo corners add to the old-time feeling of this autumnal page.

materials and equipment

- spray adhesive
- 20 x 30cm/8 x 12in rectangle of blue craft paper
- 30cm/12in square sheet of brown card (stock)
- scissors
- narrow double-sided tape
- striped ribbon
- 4 shirt buttons
- red thread and needle
- 2 portrait format photographs
- 8 manila photo corners
- reproduction Thanksgiving scraps and photocopies
- glue stick
- skeleton leaves
- check cotton fabric scraps

1 Glue the blue craft paper to the centre of the background card. Cut two strips of double-sided tape and stick them over the two joins. Peel the protective layer from the tape and stick down two 32cm/13in lengths of ribbon, overlapping 1cm/½in at each end.

2 Turn the ends of ribbon to the wrong side and stick them down. Sew on a button at each end of the ribbons using red thread. Stitch through the card as well as the ribbon and fasten off securely on the back.

3 Arrange the two photographs on the blue section of the background, then attach them to the page with photo corners.

4 If you do not have enough original scraps, you can photocopy them, adjusting the sizes as necessary. Try reversing some copies to create a greater variety of images for the collage. Cut out the images accurately.

5 Arrange the scraps on the page and glue lightly in place with a glue stick. Don't stick down the edges at this stage.

6 Slip a few skeleton leaves in among the scraps. When you are happy with the arrangement, stick down both the leaves and the scraps securely.

7 Cut out several small fabric squares, following the grain of the fabric carefully to create an accurate shape. Gently pull away a few threads from each side to create fringed edges.

8 Arrange the fabric pieces evenly along the brown section at the lower edge of the page and stick down using a glue stick, leaving the fringed edges free.

Hannukah

The lighting of candles is an important part of the celebration of Hannukah, the Jewish festival of light. For impact, use one large photograph to fill one of the pages of this double-page spread. The title is arranged over both pages and uses a variety of letter styles. Metal embellishments with a Hannukah theme are available from scrapbooking suppliers.

materials and equipment

- 30cm/12in square sheet of pale blue card (stock)
- pencil
- scissors
- scrap paper
- patterned rubber stamp
- clear embossing stamp pad
- silver embossing powder
- heat tool
- 2 x 30cm/12in square sheets of navy blue card (stock)
- spray adhesive
- die-cut machine
- large label die
- 3 metal embellishments
- pale blue sheer ribbon
- assorted chipboard letters
- glue dots

1 Draw a capital "H" on pale blue card and cut it out. Rest it on a sheet of scrap paper and stamp it randomly using a patterned stamp and clear embossing ink.

2 Place the pattern-stamped letter on a clean sheet of paper folded in the centre and sprinkle it liberally with silver embossing powder. (The paper will catch the excess powder and make it easier to pour back into the container.)

3 Using the heat tool, heat the embossing powder until it turns from powdery to shiny. Keep the tool moving to avoid scorching the card.

4 Glue the photograph in the centre of one of the navy blue sheets. Cut two 2.5cm/1in strips of pale blue card. Stick one down the left side of the page, centred in the margin. Trim the decorated initial and glue it at lower right, overlapping the photo.

5 Use a die-cut machine to cut out three labels from pale blue card. Alternatively, make a template and cut out three labels by hand.

6 Attach the metal embellishments to the tags using glue dots. Cut three lengths of ribbon to loop through the top of each tag.

7 Arrange the remaining assorted letters along the bottom of the second page of the layout to finish the title. Make sure the heavy letters are firmly secured.

8 Stick the remaining pale blue strip across the top of the second page. Place the three decorated tags in a row below it and use glue dots to attach them firmly to the card.

Mum's birthday

If the children have made a special effort to surprise their mum on her birthday, that's definitely worth recording in style. The tiny envelopes on this layout can conceal a few mementoes or additional pictures of the day.

materials and equipment

- 30cm/12in square sheet of pale blue card (stock)
- pencil and metal ruler
- craft knife and cutting mat
- pink, white, lilac, light yellow and light green paper
- glue stick
- pair of compasses
- scissors
- flower punch
- tracing paper
- white, pink and lilac card (stock)
- small coin
- eyelet punch and eyelets
- photograph
- narrow organza ribbon

1 Draw a rectangle 15 × 10cm/6 × 4in on the blue card, 9.5cm/3¾in from the top and bottom edges, and 6cm/2½in in from the right edge. Cut out the rectangle using a craft knife and a metal ruler.

2 Cut a 20 × 15cm/8 × 6in rectangle of pale pink paper. Glue the paper to the back of the card, over the aperture.

3 Cut two 5cm/2in strips of white paper to fit across the page. Glue them in place, 2.5cm/1in in from the top and bottom edges, and trim any excess.

4 Draw and cut out eight 4cm/1¾in diameter circles of paper, two each in lilac, pink, light yellow and pale green. Glue the circles to the white strips. Punch eight flower shapes in the same colours and glue them in the centres of the circles.

5 Copy the envelope pattern at the back of the book on to thin white card and cut out to make a template. Draw around it once on pink and once on lilac card. Draw around a small coin twice on to pink card and twice on to lilac card. Cut them all out.

6 On the inside of the envelopes, score the fold lines and fold in the sides and flaps. Use an eyelet punch to make holes in the envelope flaps and the pink and lilac circles. Attach the circles to the flaps using eyelets.

7 Glue the photo in place inside the aperture, leaving equal amounts of pink border all round as a frame.

8 Glue the envelopes to the left side of the page, with the flaps to the front. Fill the envelopes, then fold in the sides and flaps and wrap a length of ribbon around the circles to keep the envelopes closed.

Father's Day

You could make this layout to honour your own or your children's father on Father's Day. The little pull-out book attached to the page means that the journaling can be kept for his eyes only: get the children to write in the book.

materials and equipment

- 3 x 30cm/12in square sheets of blue card (stock)
- 29cm/11½in square sheet of burgundy card (stock)
- tape runner
- 30 x 15cm/12 x 6in sheet of Argyll patterned paper
- photograph
- scissors
- silver embossing metal
- eyelet punch
- hammer
- screw brad
- metal ruler
- medium embossing tool
- pencil
- glue dots
- 30cm/12in burgundy ribbon
- 3 pale blue buttons

1 Glue the burgundy card on to a sheet of blue card, leaving an even margin all round. Attach the Argyll patterned paper across the top half of the page. Cut out a piece of blue card a little larger than the photograph and mat the picture with it. Mount the photo towards the top left corner of the album page so that there is room below it for further decoration.

2 Cut out an L-shaped piece of silver embossing metal to make a photo corner. Use an eyelet punch to make a small hole in the centre. Push the screw brad through and bend open the fasteners. Place in the top right corner of the layout.

3 Cut a 9.5cm/3½in square of embossing metal. Lay it on top of a spare piece of patterned paper and emboss it by laying a ruler along the lines of the design and scoring with the embossing tool.

4 To make the book, lightly mark the remaining sheet of blue card at 10cm/4in intervals along each edge. Fold up the first third using the marked edge as a guide. Crease the fold.

5 Fold the remaining third back the other way to make an accordion fold.

6 Unfold and turn the card through 90 degrees. Repeat the two folds in the other direction. Unfold again.

7 You should now have nine equal squares. Using scissors, cut out the top right square and the bottom left square.

8 Fold the top left corner square to cover the centre square and crease sharply.

9 Flip the card over and repeat with the opposite corner.

10 The sheet can now be folded naturally into a square book shape, opening from left to right.

11 Attach the embossed metal cover to the front of the book using glue dots.

12 Stick a length of ribbon across the back of the book. This will be used to tie the book shut. Attach the book to your page using glue dots.

13 To complete the layout, attach the three buttons using glue dots.

Weddings

The history of wedding photography is almost as long as that of photography itself, as couples began to visit the photographer's studio for a picture to commemorate their marriage as early as the 1840s. However, the limits of technology meant that the camera did not leave the studio to cover the whole affair until the boom in weddings almost a century later.

It was not until the 1970s that the formal posed photographic style gave way to a more relaxed approach. Since then, weddings have been portrayed in a much more journalistic style, and the traditional album of posed shots is also giving way to much freer treatments, for which the skills of scrapbooking are extremely well suited. Many small reminders of the big day, such as menus, confetti and flowers from the bouquet, can now take their place in an album that captures the whole atmosphere of the wedding in a unique way.

A traditional wedding

This lovely reminder of a special day, featuring the wedding photograph and invitation, and decorated with cut-out doves and hearts, is simple yet effective in black, white and gold. This page can be the first in a wedding album, to be followed by other pictures of the happy day.

materials and equipment

- spiral-bound album
- craft knife
- metal ruler
- cutting mat
- heavy white paper
- fancy-edged scissors
- translucent glassine paper
- glue stick
- wedding photograph
- transparent photo corners
- scissors
- pencil
- gold paper
- gold card (stock)
- translucent envelope
- wedding mementoes: invitation, pressed flowers, ribbon, confetti

1 Before starting work on the layout itself, make a protective page for the treasured photograph by cutting the preceding page out of the album to within about 2.5cm/1in of the spiral binding. Use a craft knife and a metal ruler, and work on a cutting mat.

2 Cut another strip of paper slightly wider than the first strip from a sheet of heavy white paper. Trim one long edge with fancy-edged scissors. Cut a sheet of glassine paper or other translucent paper the same size as the album pages to replace the page you have removed.

3 Glue the glassine paper to the tab in the album, then cover this with the single strip of paper with the decorative edge visible. The translucent protective sheet should now be sandwiched between the two tabs. Allow to dry.

4 Assemble the photograph display. Using fancy-edged scissors, cut around the edges of a piece of heavy white paper slightly larger than the photograph. Mount the photo on this using transparent photo corners.

VARIATION: Family weddings

Many family photograph collections include formal pictures of relatives' weddings, copies of which were usually ordered from the professional photographer and sent out to guests or to those unable to attend the wedding. Often these pictures are to be found, years later, tucked into a drawer or in a box of miscellaneous prints. Yet they are an important part of your family history, as well as being fascinating glimpses of the past, and deserve to be properly presented in your albums.

If old photographs include wedding guests unknown to you, try to find out who they are from older family members and gather all the information you can about the day. The page you design can include journaling to preserve all these memories. In the case of more recent events that you attended yourself, you can include souvenirs such as the invitation and order of service.

It's nice to design the page in a way that is appropriate to the period and the style of the wedding: you can usually get plenty of ideas from the clothes worn by the guests and the settings of the photographs. Many of these will be in black and white so will look best against subtly coloured backgrounds.

5 Copy the dove and heart templates at the back of the book and cut them out. Draw round them on the wrong side of gold paper and heavy white paper. Reverse the dove motif so that they face in different directions. Cut them out.

6 To assemble the album page, stick down a piece of gold card slightly larger than the mounted photo. Add a translucent envelope containing a memento of the occasion such as an invitation, together with any other small saved pressed flowers, ribbon, confetti or similar. Place some of the motifs you have cut out inside the envelope too. Glue down the mounted photograph. Stick the dove and heart cut-outs on to the page in a pleasing arrangement.

An Indian wedding

Traditional Indian weddings are celebrated on a huge scale, with a great deal of ritual, and hundreds of guests are often invited and lavishly entertained. The ceremony is full of vibrant colour and sparkle, with splendid clothes, flowers and food, and provides plenty of visual inspiration for a gorgeous album page ornamented in red and gold.

1 Cut a rectangle of starry tissue paper measuring 30 × 10cm/12 × 4in and use spray adhesive to stick it to the sheet of gold card 7.5cm/3in from the top edge.

2 Cut a 10cm/4in square of red embroidered paper. Glue it to the tissue paper panel on the left side of the page, matching the edges.

3 Cut a length of gold braid and another of sequins to fit along the top and bottom of the panel and glue them in place. Glue the photograph in the centre of the panel.

materials and equipment

- gold tissue with star pattern
- metal ruler and pencil
- craft knife and cutting mat
- 30cm/12in square sheet of thin gold card (stock)
- spray adhesive
- red embroidered paper
- fringed gold braid
- sequin strip
- PVA (white) glue
- 10cm/4in square photograph
- thin white card (stock)
- eyelet punch
- gold, red and green flower sequins
- star-shaped eyelets
- red and green shiny paper
- heart paper punch
- thin paper in gold and red
- small photos and mementoes
- gold marker pen
- thin gold ribbon

4 To make the folders, cut three rectangles of thin white card each 16 × 8cm/6 × 3in. Lightly score a line down the rectangles, 4cm/1½in from each side. Fold the scored lines to make flaps.

5 Punch a hole in the centre of each flap using an eyelet punch. Punch matching holes in two gold flower sequins. Attach the sequins to the flaps with star-shaped eyelets. Repeat for the other two folders.

6 Punch eight hearts for each folder from red or green shiny paper. Stick the hearts to the flaps of the folders, four on each door.

7 Cut two squares of red embroidered paper and one of thin gold paper to fit inside the folders and glue them in place. Draw a heart template to fit inside the squares and use it to cut out two gold and one red paper heart. Glue them into the folders and stick mementoes or photos of the bride and groom to the gold hearts.

8 Inscribe the names of the bride and groom in gold on the red heart. Glue the folders in position on the page, beneath the border, with the red heart in the centre. Cut three lengths of gold ribbon and tie the ribbon through the holes in the sequins to keep the flaps closed.

A contemporary wedding

Using computer-printed kisses and light, bright colours, this layout reflects a modern take on a timeless ceremony, inspired by the unconventional wedding group photograph that forms its centrepiece. You could add some text to some of the panels instead of the printed kisses if you prefer.

materials and equipment

- 30cm/12in square sheet of white card (stock)
- computer and printer
- tracing paper
- metal ruler
- pencil
- craft knife
- cutting mat
- spray adhesive
- lilac, turquoise, blue, green and cream paper
- scissors
- glue stick
- heart punch

1 Print kisses on to two sheets of tracing paper. Trim the paper to size. Glue to the white card with spray adhesive to make decorative areas.

2 Cut three 30cm x 3mm/12 x ⅛in strips of lilac paper. Glue one strip down the middle of the card. Glue the remaining strips at each side of the card, 5cm/2in in from the edges.

3 Cut a selection of rectangles and ovals on to turquoise, lilac, blue and green paper. Cut them all out.

4 Assemble the layered shapes, gluing one colour on top of another.

5 Print the bride and groom's names and large kisses on to tracing paper. Trim them to size and glue them to the rectangles and ovals.

6 Punch hearts from cream, lilac and blue paper. Glue them to the rectangles.

7 Arrange the rectangles down the lilac "strings", then glue them in place.

8 Trim the photo to size, rounding the corners. Glue it in place.

Heritage wedding

A heritage treatment for an old wedding photograph requires the use of colours and embellishments that are appropriate to the period of the picture. For this layout, fabrics and flowers in muted tones create a delicate background, and the look is subtle and stylish. Pieced calico was used here, but plain undyed fabric would be equally effective.

materials and equipment

- pieced natural calico fabric
- dressmaker's scissors
- 3 x 30cm/12in square sheets of kraft card (stock)
- spray adhesive
- large wedding photograph
- 30cm/12in square sheet of cream card (stock)
- craft knife and metal ruler
- cutting mat
- wide sheer cream ribbon
- jewelled stick pin
- pen and plain paper
- cork mat
- paper piercer or bodkin
- small pearl beads
- moulded paper flowers
- dimensional glaze
- stranded embroidery thread (floss) in cream
- needle
- sticky tabs

1 Cut two 32cm/12¾in squares of calico to create the backgrounds for the pages. Cover one sheet of kraft card completely with the fabric, attaching it with spray adhesive and turning the raw edges to the back of the sheet. Cut the second fabric square approximately in half, cutting in a gentle serpentine shape, then glue it to a second sheet of kraft card, leaving the right-hand side of the card bare.

2 Double-mat the wedding photograph on a sheet of kraft card and a larger sheet of cream card. Tie a loop of sheer cream ribbon to fit over the corner of the photograph and glue it at the back. Tie the ends into a bow at the front. Stick a jewelled stick pin through the knot of the ribbon bow. Attach the photograph to the centre of the left-hand page.

3 To create the title, write the word "Wedding" or the names of the bride and groom in a flowing script on a piece of plain paper. Place the uncovered area of the right-hand page on a cork mat with the inscribed paper on top and prick evenly through the paper and the card using a paper piercer or bodkin, following the written line.

4 Attach a pearl bead to the centre of each paper flower using dimensional glaze. Use a minimal amount of glaze, and leave it to dry thoroughly before attaching the flowers to the layout.

5 Glue individual flowers down the pages following the lines of the pieced fabric, and in a line following the curved side of the fabric to cover the raw edge. Attach three more flowers to the card at the foot of the right-hand page. Stitch the title with three strands of embroidery thread, using back stitch and following the pre-pricked holes.

6 On the back of the page, secure the ends of the thread with sticky tabs rather than tying knots, as these might create indentations visible from the front.

Our wedding day

A brightly coloured wedding dress and a fun photograph were the inspiration for this jolly layout, a radical departure from traditional wedding album pages. The red bodice of the dress was decorated with bold flowers and these motifs have been repeated in the page embellishments.

materials and equipment

- 2 x 30cm/12in square sheets white card (stock)
- craft knife and metal ruler
- cutting mat
- 2 x 30cm/12in square sheets red card (stock)
- spray adhesive
- large wedding photograph
- die-cut machine
- selection of flower dies
- large and extra large circle punches
- dark pink card (stock)
- medium pink card (stock)
- foam pads
- large and extra large daisy punches
- glue pen
- rub-on letters in pink
- embossing tool

1 To make the background, trim one sheet of white card and glue it to a red sheet to leave a narrow border of red all round. Mat the photograph on red card and attach to the background towards the top right. Die-cut a selection of flower shapes and circles in red, pink and white card. Mix and match the flowers, centres and circles and glue them together.

2 Attach foam pads to the backs of some of the completed embellishments to raise them on the page. Arrange all the flowers along the left side of the photograph so that they overlap. Stick in position.

3 Punch out a selection of daisies in two sizes and in different colours.

4 Using a glue pen, stick the small daisies to the centres of the large daisies, mixing the colours. Leave to dry.

5 Place the daisies around and between the other flower embellishments and glue in position on the page.

◀ **6** Apply the rub-on letters using an embossing tool, and position the title in the lower right area of the page below the photograph. Rub on the last letter first: this will ensure that you get the spacing correct and the word will not run off the page.

BESSIE LOVE.

Family history

A heritage album is a delightful way to document your family's unique history and to preserve old photographs and mementoes for future generations. Most families have boxes of photographs just waiting to be unearthed and sorted out, and this in itself can be a fascinating journey back in time, particularly if you can ask your older relatives to help you identify the faces of long-lost family members and friends.

When you come to make selections of photographs for your pages, portraits and special occasions such as weddings and family parties will be central features, but try to include other shots that set them in context, such as pictures showing your forebears' houses or places of work, cars, gardens and home towns.

Family tree

This is a great way to record your family tree. Instead of drawing a diagram of names and dates, this family tree is decorated with pictures of each family member, glued on paper leaves with their details added alongside.

materials and equipment

- selection of family photographs or reprints
- scissors
- paper or card for template
- pencil
- paper in two shades of green
- glue stick
- sheet of marble-effect paper
- small labels
- pen
- green mount board (optional)

1 Re-photograph the pictures on sepia-effect or black and white film, or scan them and convert to monotone or duotone, ensuring that all the faces are a similar size. Cut out each portrait carefully.

2 Make a leaf template and draw around it on the wrong side of a piece of green paper. Cut around the outline. Repeat to make a leaf background for each picture, using paper in two shades of green.

3 Glue a photograph on to each leaf and allow to dry. Trim away the excess photograph to fit the leaf shape.

4 Arrange the pictures on the marble paper background, with the youngest generation at the bottom. Glue in place. Next to each photograph stick a label on which to add names and dates. If desired, mount the family tree on green mount board to finish.

FAMILY CARS

Since the early days of the twentieth century, the car has been a prized family possession. Looking back through snapshots from holidays and outings over the years, you will find they crop up in pictures of your grandmother, father or aunt just as frequently as in those of younger relatives. Sort out all the photographs featuring cars, whether they are parked at picnics, driving along distant roads or being towed away on a breakdown truck, to make a record of your family motoring.

materials and equipment

- old road maps
- photocopier
- sheet of card (stock)
- glue stick
- driving handbooks
- scissors
- selection of photographs

1 Photocopy the maps on the lightest setting. Stick them to the card to make the background, overlapping them so that all the card is concealed. Copy images of road signs from old driving handbooks or maps and cut them out.

2 Arrange the pictures on the page, leaving space at the top and centre right. Glue lines of road sign cut-outs in these spaces, on bands of coloured paper if necessary so that they show up clearly. Stick down all the photographs using a glue stick.

Victorian scrap album page

Having a formal studio photograph taken was an important event for past generations, when cameras were prohibitively expensive and required the special skills of a professional photographer to operate them. The resulting portraits – like this charming oval picture – were framed and treasured. You can update an old family photograph in this way, or print out a contemporary picture in sepia to create a period-style picture.

materials and equipment

- original or reproduction sheet of coloured scraps
- photocopier
- scissors
- oval photograph
- 30cm/12in square sheet of coloured card (stock)
- paper glue
- paper doily
- coloured paper

1 Photocopy the sheet of scraps, enlarging them if you wish. Make a second copy, this time with the image reversed (use the "iron-on" paper setting on your printer or ask your local copy shop to do this for you). Cut out each image carefully around the outline with small scissors, taking care to cut away all the white background.

2 Cut out the photograph if necessary and glue it centrally to the background. Arrange the scraps around it, placing the mirror images on opposite sides. Overlap them to form a solid border, and glue them in place when you are pleased with the results. By adding a few that break out of the frame you will give movement to the design.

3 Choose a motif from the paper doily for the corner decoration. It should be a part of the design that is repeated so that you can use it four times, and should be about 5cm/2in high. Cut out the four motifs roughly and glue a piece of coloured paper to the wrong side of each. Cut out the paper following the outline of the motif.

VARIATION: Découpage boxes

If you have a collection of small trifles and keepsakes that have been handed down to you, give them safekeeping in a pretty box decorated with Victorian-style découpage. Plain cardboard boxes ideal for this purpose are available from craft suppliers in many shapes and sizes. Cut out small reproduction scraps of flowers, cherubs, butterflies and other pretty subjects, taking care to remove any white background, which would distract from the overall colourful effect, and glue them, overlapping, all over the base and lid. Apply several coats of glossy varnish to give a rich antique look.

4 Stick one motif down near each corner of the background, pointing the designs towards the centre. Cut out eight more small matching shapes from the paper doily and glue a pair to each side of each corner shape to finish the decoration.

Remember when...

This heritage layout has a homespun look to it that suits the rustic scene in the old photograph. It has been achieved by using neutral colours, fabric, hand-stitching and twill tape printed with a nostalgic message. Photographs showing relatives at work are usually rarer than those depicting family and friends, and a good subject to record for posterity.

1 Mat the photograph on cream card. Place it on a cork mat and pierce holes, evenly spaced, all round the mat. Work a running stitch through the holes to make a border.

2 Cut a heart shape from scrap card to make a template. Iron fusible bonding web to the wrong side of the fabric. Draw round the template on the backing sheet and cut out five fabric hearts.

materials and equipment

- old photograph
- 30cm/12in square sheet of cream card (stock)
- craft knife
- metal ruler
- cutting mat
- spray adhesive
- cork mat
- paper piercer or bodkin
- stranded embroidery thread (floss) in cream
- needle
- scissors
- fusible bonding web
- patterned cotton fabric
- iron
- 30cm/12in square sheet of dark kraft card (stock)
- tape runner
- printed twill tape
- small brown buttons in two sizes
- glue dots

3 Arrange the hearts in a row across the bottom of the layout and use a tape runner to stick them in place.

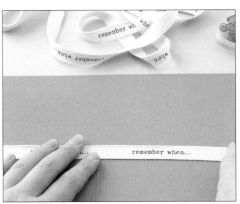

4 Cut two lengths of printed twill tape and stick them to the layout, one 10cm/4in from the top and the other below the row of hearts. Attach the photograph to the layout, gluing it over the upper length of tape.

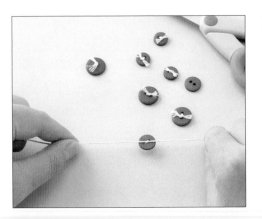

5 Tie stranded embroidery thread through the holes in the buttons. Trim to leave short ends and fluff out the strands.

6 Attach the buttons to the tape between the printed words, using glue dots, and add more buttons beside the photograph.

7 Pierce two holes on each side of and through each heart and stitch with three strands of embroidery thread.

Mother and child

This evocative sepia print of a serene mother and her robust baby boy, taken in 1909, is faded and fragile, and has to be stored carefully away from the light. To preserve the memory, it was copied and enlarged at a slightly darker setting, then cropped to remove the damaged area. The "shabby chic" style used for this layout is perfect for very old family photographs.

materials and equipment

- 35cm/14in length of fine lace, 10cm/4in wide
- scissors
- iron
- spray adhesive
- 30cm/12in square sheet of kraft card (stock)
- piece of floral-patterned fabric
- photocopier
- white A4 paper
- photograph
- glue stick
- tracing paper and pencil
- heavy pink paper
- letters and other ephemera
- 2 Victorian scraps or other pictures
- tiny paper flowers

1 Press the lace to remove any creases and trim the raw edge. Spray the wrong side with spray adhesive, and attach to the lower part of the background card with the scalloped edge facing downwards. Fold the ends of the lace to the back of the card and stick down.

2 Photocopy the fabric on to A4 paper, setting the printer to a lighter than normal setting to give a faded appearance to the design. Glue to the upper part of the background so that the lower edge lies along the top of the lace.

3 Enlarge the photograph so that it is about 17.5cm/7in high, trimming off any areas that were damaged in the original and darkening the print if necessary. Using spray adhesive, stick it down on the right-hand side of the floral paper.

4 Trace the envelope template at the back of the book on to tracing paper and transfer it to heavy pink paper. Cut out, then fold all four flaps to the centre along the broken lines. Glue the bottom flap to the side flaps.

5 Stick the front of the envelope to the layout at the lower left. Fill the envelope with letters, postcards and other ephemera, displaying them so that the stamps and addresses face outwards.

6 Glue the two scraps in place, one on each side of the page.

7 Finish off the layout by gluing a scattering of tiny paper flowers across the page.

VARIATION: Family group

For this more recent photograph of a mother and her children, a more abstract setting has been chosen, using layers of torn paper in a subtle blend of buff and brick red inspired by the marbled paper used as the background. A black border around the picture adds definition to the rather soft grey tones of the photograph, and the assortment of letters in the title includes some black and white to match the central subject.

Edwardian childhood

The formal clothing of Edwardian childhood – bonnets, buttoned boots, frilly petticoats and fitted jackets – and the strict routine of the classroom were balanced by hours spent playing in the nursery with dolls, dolls' houses, toy cars and train sets. Record this lost era with a family photograph, pages from copy books and engravings from a contemporary shopping catalogue.

materials and equipment

- hand-marbled paper
- craft knife and metal ruler
- cutting mat
- 30cm/12in square sheet of white card (stock)
- spray adhesive
- photograph
- scanner and printer
- white paper
- scissors
- gummed black paper photo corners
- photocopier
- old copy book
- glue stick
- old engravings of toys

1 Cut a square of marbled paper to fit the background sheet, and stick in place with spray adhesive.

2 Enlarge the photograph so that it measures about 16cm/6½in high. Alter the brightness and colour balances if necessary to enhance the image if it is faded. Slip four old-fashioned paper photo corners on to the picture and place it in position on the left side of the layout.

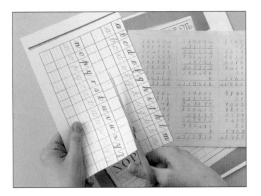

3 Photocopy and cut out four pages from an old handwriting copy book. Cut two narrow strips from one of the pages.

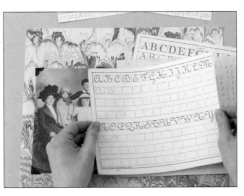

4 Arrange the other three pages on the right side of the page so that they overlap each other and the edge of the layout.

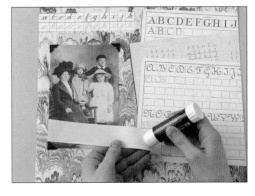

5 Place one of the copy book strips at the top and one at the bottom of the left side and glue in place.

6 Cut out engraved images of dolls, train sets, rocking horses and other toys, cutting as close as possible to the outer edges.

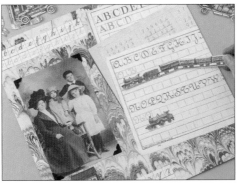

7 Arrange all the toys on the layout over the background and the copy book pages.

8 Double check the position of all the various elements and when you are pleased with the design, glue everything securely in place.

University revue

Your pictures may not always be the perfect shape for square album pages. This production photograph from a student musical sums up all the glamour and excitement of amateur dramatics, but the upright, portrait format is not ideal. With a little photocopying and clever cutting, however, a single dancer can be turned into a chorus line that fills the stage.

materials and equipment

- theatrical photograph
- photocopier
- white paper
- scissors
- glue stick
- curtain from toy theatre kit
- heavy red paper
- wavy-edged scissors
- old sheet music
- 30cm/12in square sheet of gold card (stock)
- tracing paper
- pencil
- scraps of thin black and gold card (stock)

1 Photocopy the image five times, enlarging it if necessary. Cut around the figure to be reproduced on four of the copies. Glue the pictures together so that the figures overlap realistically.

2 Cut out the printed curtain from a toy theatre kit, or cut out a paper curtain shape, and glue it to the top of the picture. Mat the picture on a square of red paper trimmed with wavy-edged scissors.

3 Cut four strips from a page of old sheet music and mount them on the back of the red paper to form a square frame. Glue to the centre of a sheet of gold card.

4 Trace the spotlight template at the back of the book and use it to cut out two spotlight silhouettes from black card and two oval discs from gold card. Glue the discs to the lights and fix in position at the top corners of the music.

VARIATION: **Period detail**

A page photocopied from an illustrated trade catalogue of the appropriate period makes a fascinating and evocative background for a heritage layout.

Family and friends

Happy times spent with your nearest and dearest are perfect subjects for your album pages, and you can include lots of informal snapshots of adults and children having fun and just being themselves – a world away from the formal posed photographs taken at special events such as weddings. For these pages you can go out armed with a camera with possible layouts already in mind, ready to look out for good subjects for backgrounds and embellishments as well as the focal points of the pages.

If you discuss your ideas with your friends and relatives you might also be able to get them to co-operate by posing together, larking about for action shots or even dressing up. If you have a digital camera you can easily take lots of pictures to give you plenty of choice at your next scrapbooking session. And if they know they've been involved, your friends will be eager to see themselves immortalized on the resulting pages.

Picnic in the park

This fun collage combines snapshots of an al fresco picnic with cut-outs of cutlery, wine bottles, plates and a picnic basket to tell the story of a good outing. This is a really enjoyable and simple way to record a memorable day; you could make similar pages about a trip to the zoo or a child's birthday party by creating collages in the same style. It's worth building up a stock of cuttings by saving promising pages from magazines with good colour photography. Alternatively, when you're snapping away during a picnic, take some pictures of small details such as the basket, rug, bottles and food, as well as general shots of your surroundings for the background.

materials and equipment

- magazine pages with pictures of picnic items
- scissors
- sheet of green paper
- glue stick
- snapshots of a family picnic
- transparent photo corners

1 Assemble the motifs for the design. Carefully and accurately cut out pictures of a picnic basket, picnic rug, plates, cutlery, glasses and food, using sharp scissors. Ensure there is no background showing once you have completed the cutting out.

2 Glue a picture of a travel rug down in one corner of the green background paper. Arrange photographs of the picnic on the paper, and when you are happy with the design, attach the pictures to the page with transparent photo corners.

3 Arrange the other cut-outs decoratively around the photographs to fill in the spaces. Some cut-outs can be placed on the rug, and others displayed in groups scattered around the picnic photographs. Glue them all in place.

VARIATIONS: Family outings

Below: Memories of childhood trips to the seaside invariably invoke pangs of nostalgia for traditional pleasures such as building sandcastles, eating ice creams and paddling in the sea, while the grown-ups looked on from their deck chairs. This digital album page captures the retro feel of those old memories by reproducing the photographs in a small square format with white borders like early colour prints. Behind them, an atmospheric photograph of a sandy beach is reproduced with a reduced opacity so that it fades into the background. A few marine embellishments complete the picture.

Above and Below: When you are portraying outings with children, include pictures of the animals or plants you saw as well as the children themselves, as reminders for them when they look at your album in future years.

Trip to the farm

In this small accordion album, photographs of a visit to a farm are mounted on tags slotted into pockets, and no child will be able to resist pulling them out to find his or her picture on each one. Close-up shots of crops and animals have been used to cover the pockets, conveying the flavour of the trip in near-abstract images that are all about texture and colour. A naive illustration created using rubber stamps provides the finishing touch.

materials and equipment

- **2 sheets of A4 card (stock)** in lime green
- tracing paper
- pencil
- metal ruler
- craft knife
- cutting mat
- self-cling unmounted stamps
- clear acrylic block
- coloured ink pads
- gift wrap or magazine pages
- glue stick
- daisy punch
- white paper
- eyelet punch and eyelets
- thin card (stock) in pale blue, turquoise and lilac
- photographs
- narrow ribbon
- gift wrap

1 Fold one green card in half lengthwise. Press the fold firmly to make a sharp crease. Trace the album template at the back of the book and transfer the tracing to the green card, matching the central line to the crease. Cut out the album.

2 Fold the card where marked to create the album. Press all the folds firmly to make sharp creases.

3 Press the self-cling stamps one by one on to the acrylic block and stamp the flower and butterfly design on the large pocket.

4 Cut sections from gift wrap or pictures cut from magazines to fit the remaining pockets and glue in place.

5 Punch a small daisy from white paper.

6 Use an eyelet punch to make holes in the corners of the pockets, and in the daisy. Insert eyelets through the holes to fix the album together.

7 Trace the tag templates at the back of the book. Transfer the shapes to thin, coloured card and cut them out.

8 Punch four daisies from white paper. Glue one to the top of each tag.

9 Punch a hole through each daisy with an eyelet punch. Trim the photos to size and glue them to the tags.

10 Cut lengths of ribbon and tie one through the hole in the top of each tag.

11 Cut two covers slightly larger than the album from the remaining sheet of card and cover them with gift wrap. Glue the covers to the front and back of the album. Trim and glue photos to the front and back covers. Cut a length of ribbon and tie it around the album to keep it closed.

A day in the garden

Summer days are often spent in the garden, having lunch or a drink and chatting with family and friends. Keep a record of this part of life by making a collage using photos of your loved ones relaxing outside, decorated with stamped garden designs and pressed flowers and leaves.

materials and equipment

- selection of rubber stamps with a garden theme: plant pots, flowers, garden tools
- selection of papers in shades of green, brown and off-white
- ink pads in black and dark green
- paper towels
- fancy-edged scissors
- scissors
- photographs
- sheet of brown paper
- glue stick
- gummed brown paper photo corners
- selection of pressed flowers and leaves

1 Stamp several versions of garden-themed designs on a selection of coloured and textured paper, using black and dark green ink. Clean the stamps between different colours with paper towels. Allow to dry.

2 Cut out some of the stamped motifs with fancy-edged scissors and others with ordinary scissors. Tear around some of the motifs to create rough edges.

For a digital scrapbook page, create the feel of a summer garden with a photographic montage in fresh greens and blues. You can find themed collections on scrapbooking websites offering suitable colourful borders and embellishments such as these jolly sunglasses, or make up your own borders and collage elements using the image-editing software on your computer. In the example on the right, all the images were cropped from one photograph, then enlarged and superimposed for a montage effect. The simpler treatment below could be achieved equally easily in digital or traditional form.

VARIATION: Summer in the garden

3 Arrange the photos on the foundation page. When you are happy with the arrangement, stick the pictures down with the photo corners.

4 Assemble the collage by adding the different stamped motifs, pressed flowers and leaves. Glue each item in position.

Gone fishing

Capture the magic of a long afternoon spent by the water's edge with this fun layout featuring a fond grandfather with his young grandson. Even if they didn't manage to hook anything with their makeshift rod, you can crop the photograph and add a catch consisting of a few embossed silver fish.

1 Cut a square of patterned paper to fit the background card and attach it with spray adhesive. Cut a 7.5cm/3in strip of dark blue paper to fit along the bottom of the page. Cut along the top edge with wavy-edged scissors and stick it in place.

2 Use the wavy-edged scissors to cut out a few "waves" from the pale blue paper and glue them at intervals across the "water".

materials and equipment

- patterned paper
- 30cm/12in square sheet of card (stock)
- spray adhesive
- craft knife
- metal ruler
- cutting mat
- thin paper in dark and pale blue
- wavy-edged scissors
- 2 photographs
- glue stick and sticky tape
- tracing paper
- fine waterproof pen
- silver embossing foil
- thick card or cork mat
- embossing tool or empty ballpoint pen
- old scissors
- large needle
- stranded embroidery thread (floss) in cream or fine string

3 Decide on the best position for the two photographs and stick them to the patterned background using a glue stick.

4 Trace the fish template at the back of the book and cut out around the outline. Cut a small rectangle of embossing foil and, using a fine waterproof pen, draw around the template, then fill in the detail.

5 Lay the foil on a piece of thick card or a cork mat and trace over the lines with a stylus or old ballpoint pen, pressing firmly.

6 Use an old pair of scissors to cut out the fish. Make another three fish in the same way, reversing some of them so that they appear to swim in opposite directions.

7 Stick the fish to the dark blue paper with a glue stick, spacing them evenly between the waves.

8 Thread a large needle with thread or fine string. Bring the needle out at the tip of the fishing rod and take it back in close to the fish, allowing the thread to loop gently. Tape the ends to the wrong side.

Birthday party

Children's birthday parties are big events to organize so it's nice to have a record of the day, as well as of your children's favourite friends, so that you can see how the the celebrations and children change as the years pass.

materials and equipment

- selection of toning papers
- 6 photographs
- 30cm/12in square sheet of card (stock)
- cutting mat
- craft knife and metal ruler
- spray adhesive
- corner cutter
- purple metallic ink pad
- 5 tags
- glue dots
- cup rubber stamp design
- flower and heart cutters
- brads
- sequins
- small floral stickers
- number template
- scissors

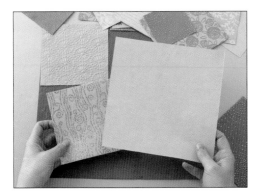

1 Choose a selection of toning papers in colours that match your photographs and the background card. Working on a cutting mat and using a craft knife and metal ruler, cut one 12.5cm/5in square and mat it to the top left-hand corner of the background.

2 Cut frames for your main photographs, 1cm/½in larger all around than the photographs. Use a corner cutter to trim the corners. Trim the photographs in the same way.

3 Tint the edge of the main photograph frame using a purple metallic ink pad. Allow to dry. Mat the photographs to the frames, then mat the frames in position on the background.

4 Choose different papers to cover each of the five gift tags. Working in a ventilated area and with scrap paper on the work surface, use spray adhesive to coat the tags and mat each to coloured paper. Allow to dry, then carefully cut each out.

5 Cut and trim three photographs and their corners to fit the tags. Cut slightly larger frames for each. Stick each of the three photographs to a frame, and a frame to a tag using glue dots or spray adhesive.

6 For a tag without a photograph, decorate a plain frame with a stamped design. Add stickers to decorate the other tag without a photograph.

7 Cut four flower motifs and one heart motif as additional decoration for the tags. Make a hole in the centre of each flower and in the top of four tags.

8 For the tags without photographs, thread a sequin on a brad, then a flower, a frame and a tag. Open out the wings of the brad. Stick the tag to the background.

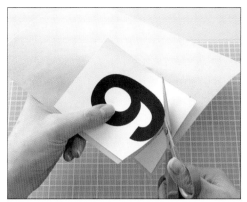

9 For the centre tag, stick a heart to the top of the frame. Decorate the remaining tags as you like.

10 Add small floral stickers to the background and the frames, as desired.

11 Cut out the child's age from coloured paper using a template. Decorate the edges with the ink pad as before. Stick in place.

Magic carpet

With a little imagination you can transform an ordinary afternoon in the garden into a fairytale fantasy. All you need is a photograph of your family or best friends sitting out in the sunshine and a picture of the hearthrug. When taking the photographs, get everyone to sit close together in a solid group, and photograph the rug from a low angle. Cut them out, mount them together on an idyllic blue sky and you have a magic carpet to take you all on a wonderful adventure.

materials and equipment

- group photograph
- computer and printer
- scissors
- photograph of rug
- hard and soft pencils
- tracing paper
- A4 sheet of thin silver card (stock)
- craft knife
- cutting mat
- scraps of coloured paper
- 60cm/24in metallic braid
- glue stick
- 30cm/12in square of sky-printed background paper
- tiny silver star stickers
- scrap of silver paper
- 4 small silver fabric motifs

1 Enlarge the group photograph so that it measures approximately 15cm/6in from side to side and cut it out, following the outline of the figures as closely as you can.

2 Enlarge the picture of the carpet to about 25cm/10in wide and cut out carefully, eliminating the original background.

3 Trace the template from the back of the book, enlarging it to 30cm/12in wide. Transfer the outline to silver card. Cut along the skyline with scissors and cut out the windows with a craft knife on a cutting mat.

4 Glue a small piece of coloured paper behind each window opening.

5 Cut two lengths of metallic braid and glue them along the top and bottom edges of the sky-printed background sheet.

6 Stick the silhouette to the background, just above the braid. Glue the family picture on to the carpet, then move it around the card until you are happy with its position. Stick it in place using a glue stick.

7 Scatter the silver star stickers across the sky. Cut out a small crescent moon from silver paper and stick it low down in the sky near the buildings.

8 Stick a silver motif on each corner, to cover the ends of the braid.

New Year's Eve

Beads, coiled wire and silver embellishments add a touch of sparkle to pictures of New Year's Eve celebrations. Lots of little ready-made ornaments are available to match this theme, so decorating the page is really easy. If the photographs are busy, keep the background simple so that there aren't too many things to distract the eye.

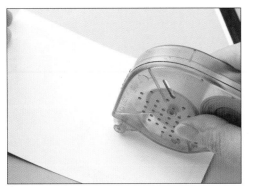

1 Cut a 30 x 15cm/12 x 6in rectangle of white card and mount all three photographs on it, cropping them a little if necessary to leave a narrow border of white between and around them.

2 Stick the panel of photographs in the centre of the black card. Punch four squares of black and white patterned papers and four squares of pale grey card and arrange them, alternating, down each side.

3 Wrap a length of wire around the dowel to form a coil. Stretch it to the length of the page, leaving 5cm/2in of straight wire at each end. Make a second coil to match.

4 Thread an assortment of small beads on to the wires. Use a generous amount as the wires are quite long.

5 Pierce holes at the the top and bottom of the layout where you wish to anchor the wires. Push the straight ends of the wires through the card and anchor them at the back of the layout with sticky tabs. Add the sticker embellishments to the plain grey squares.

6 Use a label maker to punch out a title for each photograph and the date on black tape. Stick the labels to the pictures and add the date in the corner of the layout.

materials and equipment

- craft knife
- metal ruler
- thin card (stock) in white and pale grey
- cutting mat
- 3 photographs, each 15 x 10cm/6 x 4in
- tape runner or glue stick
- 30cm/12in square sheet of black card (stock)
- black and white patterned papers
- 5cm/2in square punch
- fine silver wire
- thin dowel rod
- wire cutters
- small glass beads in assorted colours
- paper piercer or bodkin
- sticky tabs
- label maker
- black label tape

Sports

Whether your family members are active participants in sports, or fanatical supporters of a local team, sporting subjects make for rewarding layouts. This is a great theme for pages about children, where you can present them taking part in team games and school sports days, or showing off their daredevil skills on skateboards or bikes.

All kinds of games and sports make very satisfying subjects for scrapbooking pages, as they are all easily identified by the images and accessories associated with them, and there is plenty of strong colour in team strips, pitches and equipment. Add to these features the dramatic action shots you can capture in your photographs, and you can easily produce really eye-catching pages in this theme.

Cycling

This very simple double-page spread uses black ink trails to suggest the muddiness of a cycling trip in the countryside. Die-cut cog shapes and screw decorations reflect the mechanics of the bike.

materials and equipment

- black ink pad
- 2 x 30cm/12in square sheets of white card (stock)
- toy vehicle with rubber tyres
- sheet of metallic silver card (stock)
- craft knife and metal ruler
- cutting mat
- die-cut machine
- assorted cog dies
- matt silver paper
- 5cm/2in square punch
- photographs
- corner rounder
- glue stick
- paper piercer
- 5 screw brads

1 Brush the black ink pad around the edges of the sheets of white card to give the pages a "muddy" appearance.

2 Pat the ink pad on to the tread of a large wheel on a toy vehicle. Run the wheel across the card in different directions to create tyre tracks.

3 Cut two strips of metallic silver card 5cm/2in wide: these will form a band across the two pages. Using a die-cut machine, cut out a selection of cogs from the matt silver paper. Stick all the shapes to the strips, allowing some to overlap the edges and trimming them flush.

4 Punch details from photographs to create six square blocks. Round the two left-hand corners of the large photograph for the left-hand page, and the right-hand corners of a large photo for the right-hand page. Arrange all the pictures on the pages.

5 Position the silver strips under the photographs. Trim them so that the ends align with the pictures and round the corners. Glue everything in place. Pierce holes in the positions where you will insert the screw brads.

6 Push the brads into the holes and fold back the fasteners on the back of the pages to hold them in place.

Basketball

The bright colours contrast with the black and white action photographs and the repeated circle motif clearly links with the ball game but also gives a sense of motion to the pages.

materials and equipment

- circle cutter
- thin card (stock) in lime green, turquoise and deep pink
- repositionable tape runner
- 2 x 30cm/12in square sheets of burnt orange card (stock)
- scissors
- eyelet tool kit
- letter stickers
- photographs
- 2 x 30cm/12in square sheets of chocolate brown card (stock)
- label maker
- black label tape

1 Cut out circles from the lime green, turquoise and deep pink card in assorted sizes. If you don't have a circle cutter to do this you can draw and cut out a number of templates or draw round plates and cups of various sizes.

2 Apply repositionable tape to the backs of the circles. This will allow you to move them around on the layout until you are happy with their positioning. Stick the circles to both sheets of burnt orange card in a random arrangement.

3 Allow some of the circles to overlap the edges of the sheets and trim off the excess with scissors. On the inner edges of the pages, stick the circles to one side and trim, then stick the remaining parts to the opposite page, aligning them accurately.

4 Use an eyelet tool to punch out small circles around parts of the large circles. If you have different sized punches try to use them all to add variety.

5 Create the title using letter stickers. When placing these, always work from the outer edge of the page towards the middle, which will sometimes mean spelling the word backwards, to ensure that each word is accurately positioned.

6 Position the photographs so that they overlap the card circles, taking care to avoid any of the punched circles.

7 Stick the finished pages to sheets of chocolate brown card, which will show through the punched holes.

8 Use a label maker and black tape to punch the date and stick the label beside one of the photographs.

Skateboarding

Grunge and funky colours go hand in hand with skateboarding, and this double page spread has plenty of both. Inks, fabric, curly paperclips and roughly torn paper combine to create a great background for these pictures.

materials and equipment

- 2 x 30cm/12in square sheets of turquoise card (stock)
- 2 x 30cm/12in square sheets of bright patterned paper
- thin lime card (stock)
- craft knife and metal ruler
- cutting mat
- ink pads in black and red
- hole punch
- roughly torn strips of woven cotton fabric
- "S" letter sticker
- die-cut "K"
- rub-on number "8"
- 4 round paperclips
- 4 photographs
- glue stick

1 Cut both sheets of turquoise card in half. Tear away a strip approximately 4cm/1½in wide from each side, tearing at a slight angle. Always tear towards yourself to expose the inner core of the card on the right side.

2 Moisten your finger and use it to roughen the torn edges of the card strips. Roll the edges back, without trying to do this too evenly. Stick the card strips on top of the squares of patterned paper.

3 Cut four strips of lime card 6mm/¼in wide and 30cm/12in long. Roughly ink the edges of each strip using the black ink pad, then glue to the turquoise cards, aligning the strips across the two pages. Punch pairs of holes to tie the fabric strips through.

4 To create the "S" for the title "skate", use the paper frame of a letter sticker as a template. Stick it gently to the layout (so that it can be peeled off later) and stipple through it using a red ink pad.

5 When the ink is dry, pull away the template. Add the die-cut "K" and rub on an "8" to complete the title.

6 Slide a paperclip on to the edge of each photograph. Arrange the photos at random angles across the centre of both pages and glue in position.

Skiing

Photographs of sunny days on the slopes demand pages with a touch of winter sparkle. This is a very simple layout, but the combination of snowflakes with silver patterned paper and an ice blue background gives a crisp, snowy look.

materials and equipment

- silver patterned paper
- guillotine (or craft knife, metal ruler and cutting mat)
- 2 x 30cm/12in square sheets of pale blue card (stock)
- eyelet punch
- tack hammer
- 24 silver eyelets
- foam brush
- acrylic paint in cobalt blue
- 6 sparkly snowflake buttons
- large white rub-on letters
- 4 photographs
- white card (stock), optional
- glue dots

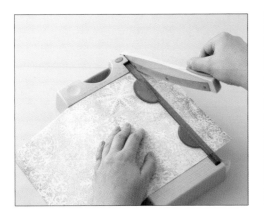

1 Cut 12 strips of silver patterned paper measuring 2.5 x 18cm/1 x 7in. If you don't have a guillotine, mark out the strips and cut them using a craft knife and metal ruler and working on a cutting mat.

2 Lay the strips across the two sheets of blue card at uneven heights and angles. Use the eyelet tools and silver eyelets to attach them to the card at each end.

3 Using a foam brush, swipe a broad stripe of cobalt blue acrylic paint across the top left and bottom right corners of the layout. Leave to dry.

4 Dab the edges of the snowflake buttons with the blue paint. This technique will make the snowflake shapes stand out more on the page.

5 When the paint is dry, rub on the white letters over it to create the titles.

6 Print the photographs with a white border or mount them on to white card. Glue them at angles across the pages and stick on the snowflake buttons using glue dots.

Tennis

If you or others in your family enjoy getting to grips with the game, make this tennis court layout to celebrate your skills. You could personalize the page by using your own club colours for the background.

materials and equipment

- 30cm/12in square sheet of green card (stock)
- 2 x 30cm/12in square sheets of purple card (stock)
- craft knife and metal ruler
- cutting mat
- spray adhesive
- photographs
- white acrylic paint
- paintbrush
- alphabet foam stamps
- 2 purple and 4 green photo turns
- paper piercer or bodkin
- 6 dark green brads
- date stamp
- black ink pad

1 Cut two wide and one narrow strip of green card and glue them vertically to the purple sheets to make the background. Glue the photographs in position on both pages. Brush white acrylic paint on to foam stamps to print the titles.

2 On the right-hand page stamp the letters in reverse order from right to left so that you do not run out of space for the title. Take care not to overload the letters with paint or it will smudge. The words "game", "set" and "match" are used here.

3 Lay a photo turn over the edge of each picture and pierce a hole in the card through the eye of the turn.

4 Push a brad through the hole and fold the fasteners down at the back of the card to anchor the turn to the page.

5 Add the date in the corner of the layout using a date stamp and a black ink pad.

School sports day

Make a first school sports day special for your child by creating a spread in your album to celebrate their determination, whether or not they managed to win any prizes. Your choice of photographs can emphasize what a good time everyone had taking part in the fun races.

materials and equipment

- large square punch
- photographs
- large dinner plate
- pencil
- 30cm/12in square sheet of patterned card (stock)
- scissors
- craft knife and metal ruler
- cutting mat
- 30cm/12in square sheets of cobalt and navy blue card (stock)
- glue stick
- computer and printer
- pale blue card (stock)
- 2 metal sports embellishments
- glue dots

1 Use a large square punch to cut out three interesting sections from your photographs. Move the photos around in the window of the punch until you find the area you want. (If you don't have a punch, cut out the details using a craft knife and metal ruler, working on a cutting mat.)

2 Draw round a large dinner plate on the patterned card and cut out the circle using scissors. Cut the circle in half and position each semicircle at the outside edge of the cobalt blue pages. Cut two wide strips of navy card and glue them next to the semicircles. Glue a strip of patterned paper at the inner edge of the right-hand page.

3 Print the title "determination" in reverse on pale blue card and cut out the individual letters using a craft knife. The letters are less likely to tear if you cut out the centres before the outlines. Take your time and make sure the blade is sharp.

4 Glue the letters up the right-hand side of the layout using a glue stick. Position the whole word first to help you space the letters evenly.

5 Mat all the photographs on pale blue card and arrange them on the layout. Print a caption on pale blue card and add it to the first page.

6 Tie the metal embellishments together with a thin strip of pale blue card and attach them to the layout using glue dots.

Family pets

Dogs, cats and other animals are important and much-loved members of many families. If you have pets, they're sure to feature often in your photographs of outings, celebrations at home, and fun and games in the garden, but it can also be rewarding to devote some special pages of your scrapbook to your animals, making them the stars rather than the supporting cast.

Animals' lives are far shorter than ours, and this is a lovely way to remember them in later years. Children usually have a special connection with their pets and love to look back at photographs of their antics, or to find out about pets that were around before they were born or when they were very small. Album pages can paint vivid pictures of your pets' lives if you include shots of them in youth and age, at play, at rest, enjoying their favourite toys and doing their party tricks.

My pet rabbit

Sometimes it's difficult to find the perfect ready-made embellishments for your pages, especially if you're working on an unusual subject. Why not make your own? Polymer clay is the ideal material with which to create easy small-scale pieces to decorate your album.

materials and equipment

- polymer clay in orange and green
- baking tray
- 2 rabbit photographs
- craft knife
- metal ruler
- cutting mat
- 30cm/12in square sheets of card (stock) in mid-green, dark green and lime
- spray adhesive
- large square punch
- green vellum
- tape runner
- rub-on faux stitches
- embossing tool
- wire cutters
- 3 rabbit buttons
- glue dots

1 Mould a carrot shape in orange polymer clay and add some green leaves. Place the carrot on a baking tray and harden in an oven according to the manufacturer's instructions. Leave to cool.

2 Crop the photographs as necessary and mount on a large piece of mid-green card. Punch out three squares from dark green card and add them to the arrangement.

3 Create the left-hand border by layering a strip of torn green vellum with a narrower strip of torn dark green card. Glue the border to the background 2cm/¾in from the edge of the page.

4 In the 2cm/¾in gap use an embossing tool to rub on a line of faux stitches, taking care that they are straight.

5 Use wire cutters to snip the shanks off the backs of the rabbit buttons. Stick one to each dark green square using a glue dot.

6 Carefully tear green vellum into oval "lettuce leaves". Stick them overlapping at the bottom of the page.

7 Attach the polymer clay carrot near the lettuce leaves. Use a generous quantity of glue dots as it is quite heavy.

Folk art cat

The colours in these photographs of a favourite cat suggested they would work well with the natural blues, rusts and ochres characteristic of American folk art. This in turn inspired the simple embellishments of cut-out hearts and paper animal shapes, and the drawn "stitches" around the woodgrain panel, which are a reminder of traditional patchwork.

1 On a background sheet of off-white paper, assemble a background collage using woodgrain design and complementary coloured papers. Cut out four triangles of patterned paper to go across the corners. Copy the templates of the cat, heart and dove motifs at the back of the book and transfer them to the back of the patterned papers. Cut them out using scissors.

2 Glue the collage elements on to the background paper. Leave a narrow border around three sides and a wider strip down one side on which to place the cut-outs. Glue the cut-out motifs in position. Attach the photographs to the woodgrain panel using brown gummed photo corners. Finish the page by drawing "stitching" lines around the edges of the collage with a black marker pen.

materials and equipment

- off-white heavy paper
- patterned papers in woodgrain and check designs
- craft knife
- cutting mat
- tracing paper
- pencil
- scissors
- glue stick
- photographs
- brown paper photo corners
- black fine-tipped marker pen

Best friend

Create a pet montage with cut-out photographs and conventional snapshots, and decorate the whole thing with fun paw prints and cute stickers. Using a combination of rectangular snapshots and cut-outs adds interest to the overall page, while the paw prints and stickers provide extra colour.

materials and equipment

- photographs
- scissors
- 2 sheets of white card (stock)
- glue stick
- selection of children's stickers of dogs and puppies
- thin card in blue and green
- craft knife
- metal ruler
- cutting mat
- rubber stamp with paw print motif
- coloured ink pads
- paper towel

1 Decide on the general layout of the album page, then work out which photographs you want to use. Either make extra colour copies or, if you have enough, cut around some of the dog images with scissors. Arrange the pictures on the plain paper then, when you are happy with the arrangement, glue all the pictures in position. Decorate with stickers of other breeds of dog.

2 For the second page, mount the two main photographs of the dog on different coloured pieces of card, then add stickers all around the photographs to frame them. If you prefer not to place stickers directly on the original photographs, use copies.

3 Decorate both pages with paw prints, either stamping a border design or making random prints at different angles. Wash the stamp between colours and pat dry with a paper towel.

Bill and Ben the goldfish

Pet fish are quiet and unassuming compared with larger animals, but are often valued family members, so give them their own moment of glory in your album with a special page dedicated to themselves. The background paper used for this layout had a squared design, making it very easy to create a scrapbook "aquarium" for this friendly pair.

materials and equipment

- craft knife
- 30cm/12in square sheet of scrapbook paper
- gold glitter paper
- bubble effect paper
- metal ruler
- cutting mat
- square patterned paper
- spray adhesive or paper glue
- pencil
- coin
- goldfish photographs
- scissors
- star tags
- printed names
- blue ribbon
- card tags
- self-adhesive shiny paper
- plain self-adhesive alphabet stickers
- patterned card alphabet stickers
- PVA (white) glue

1 Cut a panel of gold glitter paper to fit at the top of the scrapbook paper and a panel of bubble paper to fit at the bottom. Glue both of them in place.

2 Cut a thin band of square patterned paper to go on top of the bubble panel and glue in place.

3 Draw around a coin on to the photos of your fishes, positioning it over their faces. Cut out the circles and glue one to each star tag. Print out the fishes' names, trim to size and glue one above each picture.

4 Trim the large photograph to fit the central panel, then glue it to the left side of the page.

5 Add short lengths of ribbon to the star tags and glue them in position on the right side of the page.

6 Decorate five tags in assorted shapes with pieces of self-adhesive shiny paper. Spell out the word "goldfish" on the tags with alphabet stickers. Thread all the tags in sequence on to a length of blue ribbon.

7 Position the ribbon across the top of the page then tuck the ends to the back of the page and glue them down with PVA glue.

Purry puss

This pampered fellow gets a very luxurious furry page to himself. If your cat is co-operative you should be able to get him to provide a paw print in paint with which to sign the page, but be sure to wipe the paint off his paw afterwards.

materials and equipment

- spray adhesive
- 30cm/12in square sheet of thin card (card stock)
- short pile fun fur or fleece
- scissors
- coin
- pencil
- thin card (stock) in red and green
- eyelet punch
- tack hammer
- gold rub-down letters
- 1cm/⅜in tartan ribbons
- PVA (white) glue
- 3 small swing tags
- gold paper
- glue stick
- photographs
- paw print
- narrow red ribbon
- collar bell
- 3 small gold safety pins
- thin red card
- metal ruler and pencil
- craft knife and cutting mat
- 4 photo corners

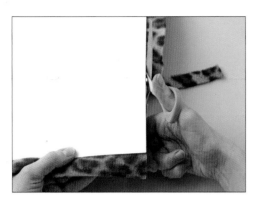

1 Spray adhesive on to one side of a sheet of card. Press the card firmly on to the wrong side of a piece of fun fur. Using scissors, trim the excess fabric from around the edges, as close to the card as possible.

2 Draw around a coin on to red and green card to make discs, one for each letter of your pet's name. Cut them all out. Punch a large hole at the top of each disc with an eyelet punch.

3 Rub a letter on to each disc to spell your pet's name, alternating the colours of the discs as you go.

4 Tie each disc to a length of tartan ribbon. Use PVA glue to attach the ribbons to the right side of the page, turning the raw ends to the back.

5 Glue three tags to the wrong side of a piece of gold paper and trim away the excess paper. Re-punch the holes in the tags with an eyelet punch. Glue a small photo of your pet to one tag, and a paw print to a second. Tie a small collar bell to the third with thin red ribbon.

6 Pin the three gold tags to the bottom left corner of the page, attaching them with small gold safety pins.

7 Cut a rectangle of red card measuring 1cm/⅜in larger all round than the large photograph.

8 Attach photo corners to the picture and and stick it to the mount, leaving an even border all round. Glue the mount to the page.

Prize-winning pony

If you have ponies that win rosettes for you or your children you'll want to honour their achievements by creating a special page. This is a very simple design using brightly coloured paper, with no other embellishments.

materials and equipment

- craft knife
- 30cm/12in square sheets of card (stock) in green and orange
- metal ruler
- cutting mat
- glue stick
- red, blue and yellow paper
- circle cutter or circular templates and pencil
- scissors
- photographs

1 Cut a rectangle of orange card measuring 29 × 10cm/11½in × 4in and glue it to the right-hand side of the green card, leaving very narrow borders of green around three sides.

2 Cut three rectangles measuring 20 × 7cm/8 × 2¾in from red, blue and yellow paper. Glue them to the left side of the page, spacing them evenly, with the yellow at the top, then red, then blue.

3 Cut three triangles 20cm × 7cm/8in × 2¾in from red, blue and yellow paper. Glue them on top of the rectangles, placing red on yellow, blue on red and yellow on blue.

4 To make the rosettes, cut three large and three small circles of red, yellow and blue card. Glue the smaller circles on top of the large circles. Cut two thin rectangles in the same colours of each paper. Snip the ends diagonally to make ribbons. Glue the ribbons to the backs of the rosettes.

5 Draw a circle around each horse's head in a small photograph and cut it out.

6 Glue a horse's head in the centre of each rosette.

7 Glue the rosettes to the orange panel on the right of the page, with the red one at the top, blue in the middle and yellow at the bottom.

8 Glue two large horse photographs to the panel on the left side of the page, spacing the pictures evenly.

Travel

Trips and vacations are prime themes for scrapbooks: everyone's feeling relaxed, you have time to take lots of good pictures and – with luck – the weather's wonderful. If you're touring there will be new sights to see every day and new experiences to inspire you. Keeping your scrapbook in mind while you're away you'll remember to hoard lots of good-looking holiday ephemera, such as tickets, menus, hotel bills, little natural objects such as shells and pressed flowers, and maybe some exotic food packaging and foreign newspapers or magazines that you can take cuttings from.

Jot down plenty of notes so that you don't forget the name of that perfect beach or what you ate at your favourite restaurant. The more detailed your journaling the more memories you'll preserve, and the more fascinating your travel albums will be for you and your family in the years to come.

Beside the sea

A summer trip to the seaside is an intrinsic part of family life. The leisurely pastimes that make up a day's outing or a week's stay by the sea – paddling, swimming, beachcombing and building sandcastles – have remained unchanged over the years, and this album page brings together snaps of three generations of the same family having fun on the beach.

materials and equipment

- graph paper
- fine pen
- ruler
- A4 sheet of thin card (stock)
- craft knife
- cutting mat
- tracing paper
- selection of colour and black and white photographs and postcards
- watercolours
- fine paintbrush
- 30cm/12in square sheet of coloured card (stock)
- glue stick

1 Using the template at the back of the book as a guide, draw the postcard frame on graph paper, leaving margins of 5mm/¼in between all the shapes and 1cm/⅜in around the outside. Cut a rectangle of white card to the exact size of this rectangle.

2 Trace each of the five segments on to a separate piece of tracing paper with a ruler and a fine pen. These templates will act as guides for selecting which images to use and where to crop them.

3 Place each tracing over your chosen pictures until you find a composition that will fit well within the outline. You may need to enlarge or reduce the photographs.

4 Black and white pictures can be hand-tinted with watercolour so that they blend in with the newer photographs. Use a fine brush to build up delicate layers of colour – without letting the paper become too wet.

5 Cut out the centre rectangle and one of the corner segments from the graph paper template. Draw around these segments on your chosen photographs and cut out around the outlines.

6 Glue the segments on to the white card rectangle, making light pencil guidelines to ensure that they are positioned correctly.

7 Photocopy and cut out other pictures that have not been used on the "postcard" then arrange these, along with the postcard itself, on the coloured card. Glue everything in place using a glue stick.

78342

Sightseeing in the States

The Stars and Stripes make a really colourful background, but this simple idea could easily be adapted using the flag of whichever country you have visited. The folded airmail envelope opens to reveal a mini-album of extra pictures.

materials and equipment

- dark blue paper
- craft knife
- metal ruler
- cutting mat
- 30cm/12in square sheet of white card (stock)
- silver star stickers
- pencil
- glue stick
- red paper
- 5 luggage labels
- photocopy of denim fabric
- hole punch
- photographs
- natural twine
- two airmail envelopes
- adhesive tape

1 To make the background flag, cut a 15cm/6in square of blue paper and glue it in the top left corner of the white card, matching the top and side edges exactly.

2 Stick 50 silver stars in nine rows to the blue square. For the first row space six stars evenly, starting 1.5cm/½in from the left-hand side, with their lower tips 2.5cm/1in below the top edge. For the second row position five stars between the stars of the first row.

3 Cut four strips of red paper 15 × 2cm/6 × ¾in, and three strips 30 × 2cm/12 × ¾in. Glue the strips to the white card to form the American flag, butting the short ones against the blue square, and leaving the same depth of white background between each horizontal strip.

4 To make the tags, remove the string from five luggage labels. Cover each label with denim paper and trim the paper to size. Make a new hole at the top of each label using a hole punch.

5 Trim a photograph to fit across the centre of each luggage label and glue in place. Tie a short length of twine through each hole.

6 To make the mini-album, fold two airmail envelopes into three. Tape the ends together to make a six-page album.

7 Trim the remaining photographs to fit the pages of the mini-album and glue them in position.

8 Glue all the tags in place on the flag page, then stick the mini-album in the centre of the lower row.

Trip to Japan

There is always something exciting about discovering a new country and its culture. Record your journey by collecting interesting ephemera as you travel; when you get back home, display it on a series of luggage labels.

materials and equipment

- patterned origami paper
- 30cm/12in square sheet of deep red card (stock)
- scissors
- spray adhesive
- photocopier
- old atlas
- emphemera including tickets, bills and wrappers
- luggage labels
- photographs
- fine permanent marker pen
- hole punch
- narrow black ribbon
- self-adhesive foam pads

1 Cut one sheet of origami paper in half, then glue one and a half sheets to the top left corner of the background card with spray adhesive, leaving narrow margins between them and around the outer edges.

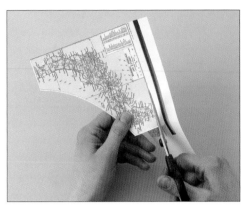

2 Photocopy a map of Japan from an atlas, reducing the size as necessary to fit into the bottom right-hand corner, and cut out, shaping the upper edge in a gentle curve. Glue in place using spray adhesive and add two tickets overlapping parts of the map.

3 Remove the string from a luggage label. Place it over a photograph and draw round the edge with a fine waterproof pen.

4 Mark the position of the hole, then cut out around the outline and punch a hole at the centre top.

5 Cut a 20cm/8in length of narrow ribbon and loop it through the hole. Make one or more additional labels in the same way.

6 Small items of memorabilia can be displayed by sticking them on to plain labels. Larger pieces, such as a calendar page, can be reduced in size on a photocopier.

7 Tie all the labels together loosely in a bunch. Attach the knot to the top left corner of the card and then anchor the labels on the page with foam pads.

Spanish memorabilia

This collection of memorabilia from a vacation in Spain is attractively displayed in a practical way, with functional pockets in which to slip airline tickets, restaurant bills, postcards and other bits and pieces picked up during the trip. A photo-montage of attractive places can be made from a duplicate set of pictures to fill another page of the album.

materials and equipment

- craft knife
- metal ruler
- cutting mat
- 4 x 30cm/12in square sheets of red card (card)
- masking tape
- pencil
- eyelet punch
- tack hammer
- small nickel eyelets
- scissors
- tickets, stamps and other travel memorabilia
- bone folder
- glue stick
- assorted paperclips
- photographs

1 Using a craft knife and metal ruler and working on a cutting mat, cut out a 12.5cm/5in square from red card and tape it in the centre of one large square of card. Mark the positions for eyelets in each corner of the small square. Punch a hole at each marked point using an eyelet tool. Insert the eyelets through both layers of card. Tickets, pictures and travel memorabilia can be slipped under the small square.

2 To make a pocket, cut a larger square of red card and attach a smaller piece to it with an eyelet. Score around two adjacent edges of the square. Trim away the corner between the scored lines and fold in the edges sharply with a bone folder to make two flaps. Glue these to a large card square. Memorabilia, such as tickets, stamps and notes can be inserted in the flap pocket or attached to the pocket with paperclips.

3 For the photo-montage, use duplicate prints or make extra copies so that you can cut them up as necessary to make an effective composition. Arrange all the photographs and other pictures in a pleasing way on the last square of red card. Trim away any unnecessary parts of the photographs using a craft knife and a metal ruler, and working on a cutting mat. Once you are happy with your arrangement, glue all the pictures in place using a glue stick.

A day in the countryside

Machine stitching on card is a very quick way to add colour, pattern and texture to your page, and you can use a variety of stitches to real effect. This simple page uses fresh colours to echo the springlike tones of the photographs.

materials and equipment

- sewing machine
- light purple thread
- scrap card (stock)
- 2 x 30cm/12in square sheets of lilac card (stock)
- pencil
- scissors
- flower-shaped punches in two sizes
- light and dark purple card (stock)
- photographs
- glue dots
- pink rub-on letters
- embossing tool

1 Thread the machine with light purple thread and do a test on spare card to get the tension right. Stitch slowly across the lower part of the page to create two gently waving lines. Align the starting points on the second page with the ends of the first lines.

2 Punch a selection of flowers from light and dark purple card using a large and a small punch.

3 Crumple the flowers to add texture. Flatten out and stick the smaller ones on top of the larger ones. Use glue dots to stick them along the lines of stitching.

4 Double-mat the photographs on light and dark purple card and glue to the pages. Rub on the title lettering in one corner.

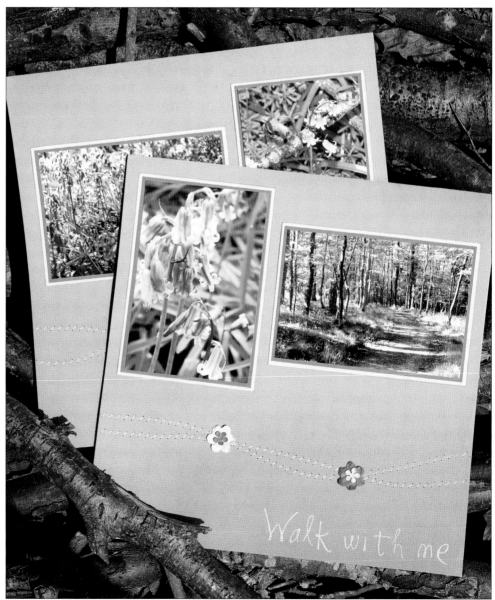

A weekend in Paris

This is an excellent way to combine a large number of photographs and your journaling on one page. The paper bag book contains pockets for mini-pages displaying more photographs as well as tickets, maps and other souvenirs.

materials and equipment

- guillotine
- photographs
- 30cm/12in square sheet of red card (stock)
- 3 flat-bottomed brown paper bags
- heavy-duty stapler
- selection of coloured card (stock)
- glue stick
- two-hole punch
- binder clip
- file tabs
- tickets, stamps and other travel memorabilia
- glue dots
- letter and number stickers

1 Using a guillotine, crop a selection of photographs into 6cm/2½in squares.

2 Arrange the photographs in a grid on the square card, using repositionable tape so that you can adjust them as necessary. Leave space for the title and the paper bag book on the right-hand side.

3 To make the book, stack the three bags together with the flat bottoms facing upwards and at alternate sides.

4 Fold the whole pile in half and make a crease at the fold. Staple along the fold to make the spine of the book.

5 Cut a piece of card to fit the height of the book and fold it over the spine. Glue in place using a glue stick. Punch two holes through the spine and insert the binder clip.

6 Cut out squares of card to fit the pockets created by the paper bags. Staple file tabs to the edges and fill the pages with pictures, ephemera and journaling.

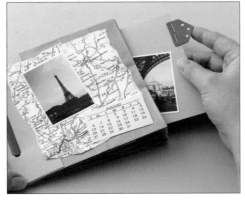

7 Decorate the front of the book and place all the cards inside the pages.

8 Attach the book to the layout with a generous number of glue dots to support its weight. Use stickers to create the title and the date.

The seasons

Though the seasons return to delight us year by year, no two days are ever truly alike, and nature is always ready to astonish us with its beauty. For photographers, the desire to capture fleeting effects of light and colour in the natural world is a powerful impulse, and successful attempts are well worth framing beautifully on your scrapbook layouts.

Pages with seasonal themes can make an album in themselves, perhaps highlighting your favourite landscapes or country walks, or tracing the annual round in your own garden. Or you can use them to punctuate more general collections of photographs, to place your family activities and celebrations in a seasonal context.

A seasonal mosaic

Photographic mosaic is a lot easier than it looks as long as you take your time and measure accurately before cutting up your pictures. Special sheets marked with a grid take care of all the spacing and lining up for you. This is a wonderful way to create an impressionistic image of seasonal flowers.

materials and equipment

- photographs
- repositionable tape runner
- cutting mat with printed grid
- craft knife
- metal ruler
- 30cm/12in square sheet white mosaic grid paper
- computer and printer
- thin card (stock) in white and mid-green
- scissors
- glue dots
- 5 metal charms with a garden theme

1 Cover the back of each photograph with repositionable adhesive. Be generous with this as it will make the cutting easier.

2 Stick each photograph to the cutting mat, aligning it carefully with the printed grid, and use a craft knife and metal ruler to cut it into 2.5cm/1in squares.

3 Reassemble the photographs on the mosaic grid. If you want any pictures to occupy blocks of squares, remember to allow for the spaces between the squares when calculating the size to cut.

4 Blend the edges of the photographs into each other a little, remembering to leave rectangular spaces for the titling as you arrange the pieces.

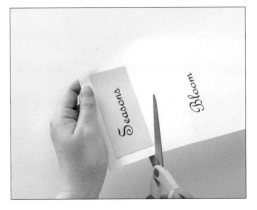

5 Print the titles on to white card. Carefully measure the spaces you need to fill on the grid and cut out the titles. Cut slightly larger rectangles from green card for the mats.

6 Mat the titles "bloom", "seasons" and "flower" and stick them in place in the spaces on the grid.

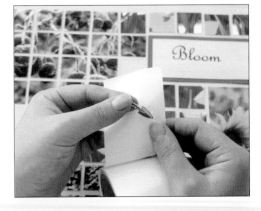

7 Use glue dots to attach the metal charms to the layout.

Spring in bloom

The bold colour scheme and geometric lines in this eye-catching picture of a tulip bed required an equally dramatic treatment. Red, green and white tracing papers, which have a translucent, matt finish, echo the colours of the flowers, and the spiral-petalled flower punch gives the finished page a strong, contemporary look. The white flower label bears the botanic name of the tulip species, but you could also use it to record the date or place where the picture was taken.

materials and equipment

- A4 sheet of white tracing paper
- 30cm/12in square sheet of green card (stock)
- glue stick
- 2 A4 sheets of lime green tracing paper
- scissors
- flower picture
- glue dots
- flower-shaped punch
- thin white card (stock)
- A4 sheet of red tracing paper
- fine marker pen or computer and printer
- pencil

1 Position the white tracing paper on the right-hand side of the green background card and glue it in place.

2 Position a sheet of green tracing paper so that it covers the lower part of the card and glue in place. Trim the edges as necessary so that they are all level.

3 Position the photograph centrally within the lime green square and stick in place with glue dots.

4 Using the flower-shaped punch, make five flowers from white card and stick them down with a glue stick to form a row down the centre of the green rectangle on the left.

5 Punch six red and six green flowers from the coloured tracing paper. Arrange them in two rows across the top rectangle, and glue in place with the glue stick.

6 Copy the plant marker template at the back of the book and cut out two green and two red shapes from the remaining tracing paper.

7 Either cut out a white label and write a name across the centre with a fine marker, or print the name. Place one of the tracing paper markers over it so that the name lies centrally, then draw round it and cut out the shape.

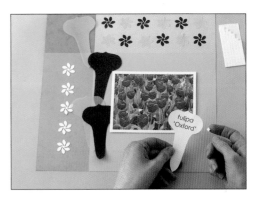

8 Arrange the coloured markers down the left side of the page and the named marker at the bottom right corner of the photograph, and glue in place.

tulipa
'Oxford'

Glorious summer

This bougainvillea-clad house, replete with peeling paintwork and faded wooden shutters, epitomizes the languid days of high summer and is a reminder of a happy holiday spent on the shores of an Italian lake. A photograph taken in the garden of the adjoining villa shared the same colour scheme: this was cut up into squares to make a mosaic-style frame, and the background was chosen to harmonize with the flowers.

materials and equipment

- transparent ruler
- pink mulberry paper
- glue stick
- A4 sheet of pale green paper
- spray adhesive
- 30cm/12in square sheet of purple card (stock)
- marbled paper in toning colours
- craft knife
- cutting mat
- main photograph, measuring 17.5 x 12.5cm/7 x 5in
- two copies of a second photograph

1 Using the edge of a ruler to give a deckle edge, tear two strips of mulberry paper each measuring about 2 x 30cm/¾ x 12in.

2 Glue one strip behind each long edge of the pale green paper so that about 8mm/⅓in is visible. Using spray adhesive, glue the paper to the centre of the purple background card and trim the ends.

3 Using a craft knife and transparent ruler, cut four narrow strips of marbled paper, each measuring 6mm x 31cm/¼ x 12½in.

4 Glue two of the strips to the top and bottom edges of the card, to conceal the edges of the other papers. Glue the remaining strips to the side edges and mitre the corners neatly.

5 Glue the main photograph to the centre of the green paper, making sure that it lies completely flat.

6 Cut the other two photographs into 2.5cm/1in squares, using a craft knife and ruler and working on a cutting mat.

7 Glue these small squares around the main picture, alternating the light and dark tones to create a chequerboard effect.

Autumn colour

The fall in New England is world renowned for its glorious display of colour. Capture the hues of this "season of mists and mellow fruitfulness" with a special album page and make your own drift of dried leaves by using a special punch to cut shapes from duplicate pictures and toning card. As a finishing touch you could make a tiny luggage tag, using the leaf punch to make the hole and threading it with garden string, to record the date and location of your photographs.

materials and equipment

- spray adhesive
- 20 x 30cm/8 x 12in sheet of heavy cream tissue
- 30cm/12in square sheet of manila card (stock), plus extra for tag (optional)
- 3 autumnal photographs, plus an extra copy of each
- manila photo corners
- leaf-shaped punch
- glue stick
- coloured paper in matching autumnal shades
- self-adhesive foam pads
- garden string (optional)

1 Spray the heavy tissue lightly with adhesive and smooth it down across the centre of the manila background card.

2 Position the three photographs on the central panel and secure them using manila photo corners.

3 Use the leaf-shaped punch to cut out a few leaf shapes from the duplicate copy of the topmost photograph.

4 Scatter these around the edges of the main picture so that they appear to be tumbling down through the sky and glue them in place using a glue stick.

5 Punch more leaves from the side and bottom edges of the other two photographs and stick them down randomly around the pictures, matching the colours.

6 Cut a few leaves from the remaining tissue paper and fix these along the bottom of the card.

7 Punch a selection of leaves from the coloured card and arrange them in a drift, with the darker colours towards the darker areas of the pictures.

8 Overlap the leaves for a naturalistic effect and use foam pads for some, to give a three-dimensional effect. Add a manila tag tied with string if you wish.

Winter wonderland

Though it may be the most monochromatic of the seasons, winter is rich in texture: dazzling icicles, the beauty of snowflakes and the dense whiteness of fallen snow. These three snow scenes are mounted on a background flecked with gold and silver leaf, and brought to life with golden snowflakes, some handmade and others from a peel-off sheet.

materials and equipment

- three wintry photographs printed with white borders
- crinkle-edged scissors
- 30cm/12in square sheet of mottled grey paper
- spray adhesive
- tissue paper flecked with gold and silver
- scissors
- glue stick
- 12 small white paper fasteners
- A4 sheet of pale blue tracing paper
- gold pen
- sharp pencil
- peel-off gold snowflake stickers

1 Trim the borders of each photograph using crinkle-edged scissors to create a decorative, frosted border.

2 Spray the background paper lightly with adhesive and cover it with metallic-flecked tissue. Trim the edges flush with the card.

3 Position the pictures on the background, overlapping and angling them if you wish to create an interesting arrangement. Glue in position with a glue stick.

4 Insert a small white paper fastener just inside each corner of the three pictures.

5 Photocopy the snowflake templates from the back of the book. Place a sheet of blue tracing paper over the first snowflake and draw in the details with a gold pen. Trace the outline with a pencil, then cut out. Make another two or three snowflakes in the same way.

6 Arrange the snowflakes in the largest space on the layout and stick them down using a glue stick.

7 Finish off the design by sprinkling a few golden peel-off snowflakes across the page.

The four seasons

These four shots of family and friends enjoying country walks reflect the changing moods and colours of the seasons. Choose papers that echo these hues for mounting and add a border of punched motifs – the simple square format pulls together the different compositions and styles of the pictures.

materials and equipment

- light green, dark green, brown and ice blue paper
- ruler
- craft knife
- cutting mat
- pencil
- 4 seasonal motif punches
- thin coloured paper
- glue stick
- photograph for each season
- 4 sheets of tracing paper to match coloured paper
- 16 small coloured paper fasteners
- 30cm/12in square sheet of card (card stock)

1 Cut a 6in/15cm square from each of the coloured papers. Pencil in five equally spaced marks along two adjacent sides of each square.

2 Using these marks as guides, punch motifs around the two sides. Choose designs that reflect the season or location of each picture – such as a snowflake for winter and a sun for summer.

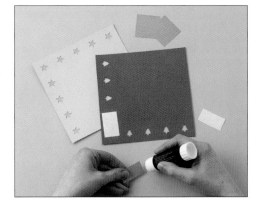

3 Choose a complementary coloured paper for each main square and stick a small piece behind each cut-out motif.

4 Glue each photograph to a piece of toning tracing paper, leaving a margin of at least 3cm/1⅛in all round.

5 Tear the tracing paper against a ruler to create a narrow border with a deckle edge on all sides.

6 Glue the photographs to their respective backgrounds so that the innermost edges line up exactly.

7 As a decorative detail, attach a small coloured paper fastener to each corner of each picture.

8 Glue the four squares to the background paper, aligning them carefully.

TEMPLATES

Copy and enlarge the templates illustrated to complete your
scrapbook album pages.

Fabric-covered box p32–33

Butterfly photograph p34–35

Butterfly photograph p34–35

Our wedding day p74–75

Family tree p78

Album page for a baby girl p40

A traditional wedding p66

Christmas celebrations p54

Mum's
birthday p60

Folk art cat p124

University revue p88

Bill and Ben the goldfish p126

Mother and child p84

Bill and Ben the goldfish p126

Spring in bloom p148

Magic carpet p102

Trip to the farm p94

INDEX

ACKNOWLEDGEMENTS

Penny Boylan, p18–19, p22–5, p30–1, p32 tint box left, p34–5, p38–9, p53b, p66–7, p92–3, p96–7, p124–5, p140. **Joy Aitman** p40–1, p58–9, p62–3, p72–5, p82–3, p100–1, p104–5, p108–19, p122–3, p141, p142–3, p146–7. **Lucinda Ganderton** p10–11, p32 tint box right, p42–3, p46–7, p56–7, p78–81, p84–9, p102–3, p134–5, p138–9, p148–9, p150–7. **Mary Maguire** p12–15, p20–1. **Sue Hallifax** p16–17, p26–7. **Gloria Nichol** p32–3. **Marion Elliot** p44–5, p50–2, p60–1, p68–71, p94–5, p98–9, p126–31, p136–7.

Thanks also to May Taylor, Claire Longdon, Cher King, Pauline Craik and Sue Davies.

Thanks to the following suppliers: Hot Off the Press, Inc., Paper Cellar Ltd, Glue Dots, Efco Hobby Products, Arty's, Fibermark, Grassroots, Magic Mesh, F. W. Bramell & co Ltd, Cretive Memories, Junkitz, and Clearsnap Inc.